The Great Gun
and the Gospel

International Politics, American Protestant Missions and the Middle East

John C. Barrett

Dr. Mitchell,
Thank you for all
your help and support.

Cover Images

© benchart - Fotolia.com

© jameschipper - Fotolia.com

Note to this edition

This edition of *The Great Gun and the Gospel*
has been privately published by the author.
Additional copies can be purchased at lulu.com.

Contents

List of Figures

List of Tables

Acknowledgments

I would like to thank all of the missionaries that agreed to share sensitive information and insight with me. Their willingness was a significant expression of trust in me and this project. I hope they find the end result helpful in their endeavors.

I would like to thank Dr. William Mitchell for his longstanding support as well as the other members of my committee: Dr. Jerry M. Long, Dr. Charles A. McDaniel, Dr. Michael W. Stroope and Dr. Donald D. Schmeltekopf. The end result was much stronger thanks to the feedback and guidance you provided.

I would like to thank Tricia Parks for her support and particularly giving me the flexibility to simultaneously pursue a Ph.D. and a career as a market analyst. I am also deeply grateful for her editing services that went above and beyond the call of duty.

Finally, I would like to thank my wife Karen and my children Nissah, Christian and William. This project required a substantial amount of time and energy and my wife made many sacrifices so that I could complete it. Your support and love are nothing short of a gift from God. Nissah, Christian, and William—I love you all very much and I anxiously wait to see what endeavors you will pursue in life.

Abbreviations

ABCFM	American Board of Commissioners for Foreign Missions
ABWG	Association of Baptists for World Missions
AGWM	Assemblies of God World Missions
AUB	American University in Beirut
AUC	American University in Cairo
BBC	Bethlehem Bible College
BFMPC	Board of Foreign Missions of the Presbyterian Church
CIA	Central Intelligence Agency
CUFI	Christians United for Israel
KDP	Kurdistan Democratic Party
KRG	Kurdistan Regional Government
IFMA	Interdenominational Foreign Mission Association
MOI	Ministry of the Interior (Israel)

NCC	National Council of Churches
NGO	Non-Governmental Organization
NSCF	National Student Christian Federation
PA	Palestinian Authority
PUK	Patriotic Union of Kurdistan
SGI	Servant Group International
SVM	Student Volunteer Movement
UN	United Nations

Dedication

To my father, my hero

Introduction

The September 11, 2001 terrorist attacks shattered the notion that religion was a minor factor in modern international relations. Realism, the prevailing theory after World War II, held that national self-interest chiefly explained international relations. "The main signpost that helps political realism to find its way through the landscape of international politics is the concept of interest defined in terms of power."[1] The terrorist attacks challenged that assumption and left theorists, academics, and practitioners alike searching to fit these events into new or adapted theories.

Prior to the attacks, several scholars offered theories of international relations that incorporate religion. Political scientist Samuel Huntington proposed the "Clash of Civilizations" thesis—that cultural differences, among which religion was the most prominent, explain international conflict. Nations with different religious foundations are more likely than those with a common foundation to settle their differences violently.[2] Sociologist Mark Jurgensmeyer believes separation of church and state is the key variable determining religion's role in international affairs. Separation in the form of secular government is a Western ideal pressed onto non-Western states from above. "Religious nationalism" was reasserting itself over "secular nationalism" in response.[3] Political theorist Benjamin Barber argues that the chief axis for conflict is a clash between homogenized global culture (McWorld) and an array of local, traditional cultures (jihad).[4] Sociologist Peter Berger built on Barber's idea and suggests there is not just one global culture emerging but four: a global popular culture (McWorld), a global business culture, a global academic culture, and a global Christian culture created by the spread of Evangelicalism.[5]

The political implications of Berger's fourth "globalization"—the evangelical missions movement—have received little academic scrutiny. Researchers Steve Brower, Paul Gifford, and Susan Rose argue that the missions movement is not just changing the global religious landscape but the economic and political landscape as well and in very dangerous ways. "Christian fundamentalism, not Islam, may have the potential to create more conflict internationally, for it can avail itself of all the advantages and power generated by a Western-dominated economic system and its invasive message of consumption."[6] Conversely, researcher Arturo Fontaine Talavera examined evangelical Protestantism in Chile and concluded it was having a beneficial impact.[7] Theologian Harriet Harris asserts that evangelical theology actually inhibits political activism its propensity to cause political instability.[8]

The paucity of research on the missions movement and its political implications is unfortunate because, as an area of study, it should provide valuable insight on the interplay between religion and international politics. All of the above theories predict political conflict when religions collide. Efforts to extend the religious foundation of one civilization into another would be the tip of the spear in Huntington's *Clash of Civilizations*. Missionary schools in the Middle East encouraged Jurgensmeyer's secular nationalism by teaching Western political and social values.[9] Barber's *Jihad vs. McWorld* conflict is clearly evident in the contrast between American missionaries and foreign cultures.

The Great Gun and the Gospel analyzes a crucial intersection between religion and international relations. Moreover, I focus on the most volatile of contexts: American attempts to spread Protestant Christianity to the Middle East. I seek to answer the question "What is the relationship between religion and international relations within the context of American Protestant mission work in the Middle East?"

Unfortunately, the macro theories offered by Huntington, Jurgensmeyer, and Barber do not serve as a suitable framework for a micro-level, case study on religion and international relations. These theories generalize global trends while my aim is to investigate and analyze specific events, organizations, and interactions. I therefore set aside these theoretical constructs and focus on more tangible and practical elements, namely:

- In what ways did political events impact mission work in the Middle East?
- In what ways did mission work in the Middle East impact political events?

In other words, I examine the record and identify, on both sides of the relationship, concrete areas of influence and consequence. I have also investigated the theological and strategic doctrines of American mission organizations in order to understand the impact of their underlining religious beliefs. This is important because the humanitarian efforts of American mission organizations bear resemblance to the humanitarian efforts of secular NGOs. Both types of organizations offer services and assistance in the fields of education, health care, and economic development. In order to clearly understand the interaction between religion and politics, it is necessary to distinguish between the evangelical work of mission organizations ("Christianizing") and the humanitarian work of mission organizations ("civilizing").[10] It is also important to understand how the underlying theology of mission organizations influences how they engage in both evangelical and humanitarian work.

My research topic posits an ideal case in which religion and politics intersect for multiple reasons. American Protestants are representative of the global, Christian, missions movement because they form the heart of it and have done so since the 20th century. As of 2001 there were an estimated 27,000 Christian missionaries working in Muslim countries, and among them roughly 1 in 2 is American. The total number, moreover, has doubled since 1982.[11] American culture represents Barber's "McWorld" phenomenon more so than any other. American political and military power is preeminent and the country has strong strategic interests in the region. The Middle East, for its part, is the best representative of Barber's "jihad" phenomenon. Nowhere is religious conversion more controversial. Nowhere does Western evangelicalism clash with the regional religious tenets more sharply. Charles Kimball, the former director of the Middle East Office at the National Council of Churches has warned, "The region is at a pivotal and volatile juncture, and it is arguably not the time for groups coming in, like someone with a lighted match into a room full of explosives, wearing Jesus on their sleeves."[12]

Scope

My research and analysis is limited to Protestant mission organizations. These encompass the many varieties of American Protestantism that exist today including mainline, evangelical, and charismatic denominations. Admittedly, there are substantive differences between these groups in terms of theology and practices. Placing all of them under the heading of "Protestantism" is not without challenges and pitfalls, but it is methodologically necessary. For one, these distinctions arose after the first wave of mission effort which sharply declined during the 1930s. Retroactively applying them is therefore anachronistic. Secondly, most of the second wave mission organizations operating in the Middle East are non-denominational and employ individuals from a variety of Protestant backgrounds. It would be misleading (if not impossible) to definitively categorize most organizations into one of the sub-groups within Protestantism. Given these challenges, I have simply included all Protestant organizations in my analysis regardless of the denominational tradition from which they are drawn.

My analysis of historical mission work in the Middle East emphasizes the years between 1880 and 1930—the time when these efforts reached their pinnacle—and covers events related to six people groups: Arabs, Armenians, Bulgarians (who lived under Ottoman rule), Jews, Assyrians, and Turks.[13] Three key mission organizations are examined: The American Board of Commissioners for Foreign Missions (ABCFM); the Board of Foreign Missions of the Presbyterian Church (BFMPC); and the Student Volunteer Movement (SVM). The first two were, by far, the largest American Protestant mission organizations active in the Middle East from 1880 to 1930; the latter was a crucial source of missionary recruits. In addition, the key educational institutions founded by missionaries are examined: The American University of Beirut (AUB) (established in 1863 as the Syrian Protestant College), The American University in Cairo (AUC) (established in 1920), and Bosphorus University (established in 1863 as Robert College).[14] This review of historical mission efforts to the Middle East highlights occasions where mission work influenced (or at least attempted to influence) international relations and vice versa. It describes the historical relationship between religion and international relations.

My analysis of contemporary "second wave" efforts focuses on efforts to evangelize three people groups: Iraqi Kurds, Iranians, and Palestinians. These groups represent key political flashpoints within the region and areas where the United States plays a particularly strong political role. Iraq is the location of the recent military intervention. Iran is where the U.S. is most likely to engage in future military operations. Israel/Palestine is the home of the Mid-East conflict.[15]

The Great Gun and the Gospel covers a considerable time span and, in many places, a few paragraphs cover events which themselves could be the subject of an entire work. Yet my goal is not to create a definitive history of American Protestant mission work in the Middle East or a definitive history of mission work and politics in the region. Instead, my goal is to investigate the relationship between religion and international relations within a case study of American Protestant mission efforts in the Middle East—a context in which both religious and political sensitivities are high. Moreover, my aim is to identify a collection of events indicative of a general trend rather than just a few isolated examples.

Methodology

Methodologically, the historical overview synthesizes diverse secondary works that touch on American mission work in the Middle East. Most are drawn from the field of history and I am particularly indebted to Joseph Grabill's *Protestant Diplomacy and the Middle East.* His work describes in great detail the influence American Protestant missionaries had on U.S. foreign policy during World War I. The synthesis of such historical works is combined with an analysis of primary sources including books, annual reports, and articles produced by the missionaries as well as comments and events documented by periodicals.

The analysis of contemporary efforts mirrors, in approach, the analysis of historical efforts, but the number of published contemporary secondary works is a recognized limitation. Few have written on contemporary mission efforts in the Middle East because missionaries today, unlike their forbears, maintain a very low profile. It is challenging to even identify where mission organizations are specifically operating. Christian evangelism is extremely controversial in the Middle East; both the missionaries and their converts have strong (and justifiable) concerns about their physical safety and security. For this same reason, few primary documents are available. The missionaries infrequently publish accounts of their experiences; periodicals rarely record relevant comments and events; and mission organizations provide scant details on their work. I therefore supplement the limited number of published materials with forty-three personal interviews. Interviews were conducted face-to-face or over the telephone. An interview guide acted as a rough framework for the discussions. However, the exact questions posed varied to focus on the more insightful aspects of the conversation. All of the interviewees were Protestant Christians involved with American mission work to the Middle East. Most were actively involved with mission work at the time of the interview; some had retired prior to the interview. Characteristics of the interviewees follow:

- Thirty-six were male; seven were female;
- Ten were born outside the United States;
- Six interviews were missiologists at academic institutions and among these, all but one taught at Protestant seminaries;[16]
- Most interviewees serve or served with non-denominational organizations (see Table 1);
- Almost all interviewees were U.S. citizens.

In order to respect the security concerns of the respondents, specific names and organizations must remain anonymous.

Comments and publications from missionaries are often used to identify the ways international politics influence mission work. For example, many missionaries active in Northern Iraq report that the Kurds were more open to Christianity because of a positive association between it and the U.S. military intervention.

Table 1 Denominational Affiliation of Mission Organizations

Denominational Affiliation of Mission Organizations	Number of interviewees
Non-Denominational	27
Baptist	11
Charismatic*	2
Mennonite	2
Methodist	2
Reformed	1

Source: Author Interviews
*Note: These two interviewees worked with mission organizations not "officially" affiliated with Charismatic denominations, but they did self-identify their organizations with Charismatic doctrines and practices.

However, quantifiable data capable of verifying the claim is not available. Statements such as the one above are thus simply presented at face value. The missionaries themselves are generally used as the judges about when and where international politics influence their work.

Defining a "missionary" is problematic yet obviously crucial to the analysis. During most of the 1800s, the term referred to individuals seeking to Christianize and "civilize" foreign cultures and peoples. The former goal meant religious conversion; the latter goal the establishment of Western-style educational, health, political, and economic systems. Mission organizations undertook both efforts and were open about their religious motivations.

During the 1900s the missions movement split into many camps according to their focus and beliefs:

- Theologically liberal organizations that de-emphasized religious conversion and became secular in character;
- Theologically liberal organizations that de-emphasized religious conversion but maintained an explicit religious affiliation;
- Theologically conservative organizations that focused on humanitarian work but also emphasized religious conversion as a goal;
- Theologically conservative organizations that focused on religious conversion and maintained an explicit religious affiliation; and
- Theologically conservative organizations that (for tactical reasons) obscured their religious affiliation but emphasized religious conversion as a goal.

Some organizations (including both liberal and conservative ones) continue to use the term "missionary" while others have abandoned it in favor of "church worker," "humanitarian worker," or similar terms.

For the purposes of analysis and discussion, I have simply reverted to the term "missionary" and its original meaning. That is to say, explicitly religious organizations that engage in international humanitarian or evangelistic work are considered to be "mission" organizations and their employees "missionaries." In addition, organizations that engage in such work but eschew religious affiliations for tactical reasons are counted as mission organizations. I have not differentiated between organizations that seek religious conversions and those that do not because the effort usually varies by degree and the individual in question. Some of those working for liberal organizations are evangelistically minded; some of those working for conservative organizations are not. This definition includes all of the aforementioned camps with the exception of theologically liberal organizations that have become secular in all but name. For expediency's sake, I repeatedly use the term "missionaries" in specific reference to American Protestant missionaries. Non-American and non-Protestant missionaries are outside the scope of my work.

Structure

Chapter One contains the analysis of historical mission work to the Middle East. It begins with an overview of its origins and growth and then discusses its underlying theology and strategy. The latter is important because theology has political implications. The impact of mission work on international politics during this time period is then gauged through an analysis of work among the six most significant people groups: Arabs, Armenians, Bulgarians (who lived under Ottoman rule), Jews, Assyrians, and Turks. Next the reverse influence is analyzed, that is, the impact of international politics on mission work. Within this section lies a discussion of the decline and end of first wave efforts which, as will be seen, were tied to political events.

Chapters Two through Five comprise the analysis of contemporary mission work. Chapter Two contains a broad overview of the similarities and differences between historical and contemporary work as well as a discussion of the theology underlining contemporary efforts. Chapters Three, Four, and Five contain the three case studies on Iraqi Kurds, Iranians, and Palestinians. Each of these chapters begins with an overview of mission work to the people group followed by an analysis of the influence of mission work on international politics and then an analysis of the influence of international politics on mission work. Finally, I present my findings and conclusions in Chapter Six.

Conclusions

My findings indicate American Protestant missionaries only have a minor *direct* influence on international politics. Their political lobbying efforts rarely yield substantive results and lobbying typically advocates for the native people-groups. This is true even when domestic churches hold political views contrary to the missionaries. For example, missionaries working among the Palestinians have challenged American churches to re-think their strong pro-Israel view of the Mid-East conflict.

Indirectly, missionaries have a much larger political influence through their educational efforts. The colleges and universities founded by missionaries become hubs of political activism. The political movements emanating from them, however, are not necessarily pro-American or pro-Christian. They express the political desires of the native people-groups which often run contrary to American or Western interests. Interestingly, the evangelistic efforts of missionaries have little-to-no local political influence. Most of the local population rejects the religious views offered by the missionaries even if they accept their political and economic views.

International politics has a far greater influence on mission work than the latter has on the former. International politics directly influences mission work by opening and closing windows of opportunity. During times of war mission work usually halts because supplies and personnel cannot reach the mission field. During times of peace mission work can be resumed.

International politics also has a substantial, indirect influence on mission work. Political repression by Muslim leaders (including nominal ones like Saddam Hussein) reportedly makes the native populations more receptive to mission work.[17] International conflict, moreover, has greatly impacted the missions movement by questioning its underlying religious assumptions. To conclude, my overall thesis is that international politics has a far greater impact on American Protestant missions to the Middle East than the latter has on the former. Moreover, the greatest political consequence of the missions movement stems from its social rather than evangelistic work or even the direct attempts to lobby policymakers.

[1] Hans J. Morgenthau, *Politics among Nations: The Struggle for Power and Peace*, 4th ed. (New York: Alfred A. Knopf, 1967), 5.

[2] Samuel P. Huntington, *The Clash of Civilizations and the Remaking of World Order* (New York: Touchstone, 1997).

[3] Mark Jurgensmeyer, *The New Cold War?: Religious Nationalism Confronts the Secular State* (Berkley: The University of California Press, 1993).

[4] Benjamin Barber, *Jihad vs. McWorld: How Globalism and Tribalism Are Reshaping the World* (New York: Ballantine Books, 1996).

[5] Peter L. Berger, "Four Faces of Global Culture," *The National Interest 49*, (Fall 1997).

[6] Steve Brouwer, Paul Gifford, & Susan D. Rose, *Exporting the American Gospel: Global Christian Fundamentalism* (New York: Routledge, 1996), 9.

[7] Arturo Fontaine Talavera, "Trends Towards Globalization in Chile," in *Many Globalizations: Cultural Diversity in the Contemporary World*, edited by Peter L. Berger and Samuel P. Huntington (Oxford: Oxford University Press, 2002).

[8] Harriet Harris, "Theological Reflections on Religious Resurgence and International Stability: a Look at Protestant Evangelicalism," in *Religion and International Relations* edited by K. R. Dark (New York: St. Martin's Press Inc., 2000).

[9] Geographically, *The Great Gun and the Gospel* focuses on modern-day, Iraq, Iran, Israel-Palestine, Syria, and Turkey. References to the "Middle East" generally refer to this geographical area.

[10] During the first wave of missionary efforts, the term "Civilizing" was used to refer to humanitarian work and the term "Christianizing" was used to refer to evangelical work.

[11] David Van Biema, Perry Bacon Jr. and Cajmes Carney, "Religion: Missionaries Under Cover," *Time Magazine*. June 30th, 2003. http://www.time.com/time/magazine/article/0,9171,1005107,00.html

[12] Ibid.

[13] At the time, Assyrians were referred to as Nestorians or Syrians. For simplicity's sake, I have consistently used to the term Assyrian which is more widely used at present.

[14] Notably, Baylor University has an exchange program with Bosphorus University. http://www.baylor.edu/study_abroad/index.php?id=52876

[15] "Palestine" is used here and elsewhere to denote the West Bank and Gaza Strip.

[16] All six interviewees serving at academic institutions had also personally participated in mission work in the Middle East.

[17] This relationship cannot be statistically verified given the paucity of data, however, it was consistently reported by interviewees.

Chapter 1: Historical Missions

Big movements often have small beginnings. The first American missionaries to the Middle East set out in 1819. By 1925 there were over 200 missionaries in the region and these individuals were just a part of a broader global effort that encompassed over ten thousand missionaries, nearly a hundred sponsoring organizations, and millions of dollars in expenditure.[1] How did such a phenomenal social movement begin? The roots of America's missionary efforts to the Middle East trace back to an inconspicuous event occurring in Williamstown, a small rural community in northeast Massachusetts. In August of 1806 five students from Williams College, Samuel Mills, James Richards, Francis Robbins, Harvey Loomis, and Byram Green, met along the banks of the Hoosack River to discuss mission work. The topic of the day was Asia and the need to send Christian missionaries to the East. It was neither their first nor their last meeting, but on this particular occasion, a sudden storm forced the group to take cover at a nearby haystack. During the ensuing thunder, lightning, and rain, Samuel Mills passionately argued that Christian missionaries should go to the East and share the

Gospel. Harvey Loomis objected and argued that the East must first be civilized before it could be Christianized. The other students sided with Mills and together they prayed that the Gospel message of Christ would be brought to the East.[2] The storm subsided, but the four students' missionary aspirations lingered on.

In 1808 the students formed a group dedicated to mission work known as "The Brethren." Samuel Mills helped expand the group to Andover Seminary when he began studies there. The Brethren grew in number and in 1810, four of its members, including Mills, offered themselves as missionaries to the Congregational General Association of Massachusetts. The next day the Association formed the American Board of Commissioners for Foreign Missions (ABCFM) to help the young men realize their goal. In 1812, six years after the Haystack Prayer Meeting, the ABCFM dispatched its first missionaries. It eventually became America's largest missionary organization; at its peak, it fielded over 150 missionaries in the Middle East alone.[3]

The Haystack Prayer Meeting and the founding of the ABCFM were expressions of broader religious movements underway in the United States at that time. The Second Great Awakening—a wave of Christian revivals and rapid church growth—was sweeping the nation during the 1800s. The newfound passion to go East and share the Gospel was a natural extension of growing religious fervor at home. More specifically, the rise of the American Christian missions movement was connected to the development of New Divinity theology. The Congregational and Presbyterian churches that accounted for the bulk of all missionaries sent to the Middle East held Calvinist theological views. Yet within Calvinism was a doctrinal tension between the belief that people are morally accountable for their choices and yet unable to accept the Gospel without divine predestination. An emphasis on the latter belief often undermined enthusiasm for mission work. New Divinity theology stressed both and provided a fresh theological argument for engaging in missions.[4]

Other distinctive characteristics marked the American missions movement. The geographical center was in the Northeast United States and Boston in particular. The missionaries were young; typically in their 20s and early 30s. They were often from rural New England towns. They were well educated hailing from schools like Middlebury, Amherst, Yale, and Princeton. Andover Theological Seminary was the key center for missionary training and recruitment.

These young men and women principally served as missionaries through one of five key organizations: the ABCFM, the Board of Foreign Missions of the Presbyterian Church (BFMPC), the Southern Methodist mission board and the mission boards of the northern Baptists and Methodists. Of the five the ABCFM was the first and largest board. It originally represented not only Congregationalist churches but also Presbyterian, Dutch

Reformed, and German Reformed churches. The latter three denominations eventually left to form their own boards, yet even then, the ABCFM continued to be the largest player in American missions.[5] One other institution, the Student Volunteer Movement (SVM), also played a pivotal role in the American mission effort. Between 1870 and 1890 the number of Americans attending college tripled.[6] The SVM was founded in 1886 during this period of growth and originated in a series of student Bible study conferences led by the popular evangelist D. L. Moody. The SVM did not directly send out missionaries but recruited students to work through established mission boards. By 1920 8,742 SVM recruits had served and far more had pledged a willingness to serve. The SVM expressed "a major late nineteenth century social movement" and helped fuel the growth of American mission work.[7]

Chronologically, the major thrust of missionary effort occurred from 1880-1930—a fact underscored by mission statistics.[8] The number of mission organizations grew from just 16 in 1860 to approximately 90 in 1900 with the aforementioned SVM representing a key addition to the field.[9] The number of American missionaries also grew from a small base in 1880 to over 9,000 in 1915.[10] Moreover, the number tripled in the first ten years the SVM began recruiting missionaries (1889-1899).[11] It was during this time period that the United States displaced Britain as the leading missionary nation and accounted for roughly one-half of all Protestant missionaries world-wide.[12]

These statistical indicators were also indicative of the culture of the time period. Missions have always been the work of a small minority and yet these decades were a time when the American public "took missions to their hearts."[13] Missionaries were a major, authoritative source of international news and leading experts on foreign countries. Mission organizations held considerable clout in Washington.[14]

American mission organizations eyed the Middle East soon after they were founded. The ABCFM's first missionaries sailed for India because the power and presence of the British East India Company offered protection and transport. Yet it also found the Middle East an alluring target because it is the birthplace of Christianity and the location of many expectant prophecies including the second coming of Christ. In 1819, under the direction of the ABCFM, Pliny Fisk and Levi Parsons set out as America's first missionaries to the region. Early efforts met with hardship, failure and death. Conditions in the field were harsh and access to medical assistance limited; both Fisk and Parsons had died of illness by 1825. Eli Smith, another early missionary, noted that "enfeebled health and shortened life are among the sacrifices necessary to work on the missions."[15] An estimated one-third of all American missionaries who went to the Middle East between 1821 and 1846 died while on duty, most of them shortly after arriving.[16] A small missionary graveyard in Mt. Seir, Iran, illustrates the efforts and challenges of the work.

Of the fifty-nine gravesites, forty-one are for missionary children who did not live past the age of three.[17]

Despite initial setbacks, missionaries had established a considerable, permanent, presence in the region by the 1900s. It was concentrated in three areas and principally directed by two organizations. In Anatolia, the ABCFM had 166 missionaries with 137 churches and just fewer than 14,000 communicants at its peak before World War I.[18] In Iran, the BFMPC had 36 missionaries, 35 churches, and over 3,000 communicants; in Syria it had 31 missionaries, 34 churches, and just fewer than 3,000 communicants.[19] The United Presbyterian Board was also active in Egypt and the Dutch Reformed Board had a tiny Arabian Mission in the Persian Gulf that included Samuel Zwemer, one of the most renowned American missionaries to the Middle East.[20]

In addition to the churches and communicants were an even larger number of schools and students. American Protestant missionaries pursued twin goals of Christianizing and civilizing the Middle East. Efforts to educate the population bore more fruit than efforts to convert them. In Anatolia, the ABCFM operated 387 primary schools, 50 secondary schools, 9 colleges, and 4 theological schools. In total these schools had over 25,911 students. In Iran, the BFMPC had 120 schools (of varying types) and over 4,000 students; in Syria it had 113 schools and approximately 5,600 students.[21] Many of the colleges and universities founded by missionaries during this time are prominent schools today, including the American University in Cairo, the American University of Beirut, Bosphorus University, Tarsus American College, the International College in Beirut, and Anatolia College (now in Greece).

Theology and Strategy

In order to understand the American missionary movement and its interaction with international politics, it is necessary to understand the theology and strategy underpinning the movement. One key characteristic was its interpretation of the millennial prophecies presented in Chapter 20 of the Book of Revelation. These passages refer to a 1,000 year reign by Christ and his followers and there are three general interpretations: *pre*-millennial interpretations hold that Christ will return prior to this millennial reign, *post*-millennial interpretations hold Christ will return after this period, and *a* millennial interpretations which believe the 1,000 year reign is symbolic rather than literal. As missiologist David Bosch writes, "From the beginning there was an intimate correlation between mission and millennial expectations."[22] Post-millennial interpretations heavily influenced the early missionaries and many foresaw a coming epoch of reason, peace, and godliness that would pervade the earth prior to Christ's return. Mission work, per this view, would inevitably succeed because the Bible had declared Christianity would reign supreme during the millennium. Missionary efforts, moreover, could hasten the coming of this epoch. Samuel

Hopkins, the principle proponent of New Divinity theology and author of the post-millennial work *A Treatise on the Millennium,* confidently declared, "Only the extension of Christian love could bring nearer to humankind the millennium that would wipe out poverty, injustice, and oppression."[23] The missionaries' eschatological beliefs thus infused a sense of urgency into their work. The millennium was in grasp if the missionaries would reach for it. Significantly, the rallying cry and goal of the SVM was, "The Evangelization of the World in this Generation."[24]

A second key characteristic of the missionaries' strategy was its emphasis on evangelizing and revitalizing the Maronite, Armenian, and Assyrian Christians in the Middle East. These groups, although holding theological views that differed greatly from American Protestants, traced their roots back to the days of the Apostles and had survived as a religious minority under Muslim rule for centuries. The missionaries initially hoped to assist them while working towards their primary goal of converting Jews and Muslims.[25] Efforts to convert non-Christians bore little fruit, however, and the missionaries came to believe that the practices and doctrines of the local Christian populations were to blame.[26] By the 1830s, they had shifted their strategy to emphasize the region's Christians. They hoped to ignite a Protestant reformation within these churches that would eventually spread the Gospel fire to non-Christians in the region. The strategy was dubbed the "Great Experiment." Rufus Anderson, the influential Foreign Secretary for the ABCFM from

1826 to 1866, explained the logic and strategy in his *History of the Missions of the American Board:*

> We may not hope for the conversion of the Mohammedans, unless true Christianity be exemplified before them by the Oriental Churches. To them the native Christians represent the Christian religion, and they see that these are no better than themselves. They think them worse; and therefore the Moslem believes the Koran to be more excellent than the Bible.
>
> It is vain to say, that the native Christians have so far departed from the truth that they do not feel the power of the Gospel, and that therefore the immorality of their lives is not to be attributed to its influence. The Mohammedan has seen no other effect of it, and he cannot be persuaded to read the Bible to correct the evidence of his observation, and perhaps also of his own painful experience.
>
> Hence a wise plan for the conversion of the Mohammedans of Western Asia necessarily involved first, a mission to the Oriental Churches. It was needful that the lights of the Gospel should once more burn on those candlesticks, that everywhere there should be living examples of the religion of Jesus Christ, that Christianity should no longer be associated in the Moslem mind with all that is sordid and base.[27]

The relationship between the missionaries and the existing native churches had highs and lows. Many of the earliest missionaries engaged in sharp theological disputes with the local churches. In 1823, the Maronite Patriarch pronounced anathema on all Protestant missionaries and their converts and one of the missionaries' first prized converts was actually arrested and tortured to death by Maronite Christian authorities.[28]   After 1830 and the shift towards the "Great Experiment" strategy, efforts were more conciliatory and the missionaries encouraged native Christians to be active members of their traditional churches.[29] As might be expected, the local churches did not welcome the missionaries' "help." In 1841, the Maronite patriarch unsuccessfully lobbied the Ottoman government to ban missionaries from the Empire.[30] In 1846, the Armenian Patriarch pronounced anathema on Protestants.[31]

On the other hand, the missionaries and the native churches occasionally found common ground when conflicts arose with Muslims. In 1860, for example, a civil war erupted between the Maronites and the Druze, a heterodox off-shoot of Shia Islam. The Druze massacred Maronites during the conflict and Western Protestants responded with an outpouring of sympathy.[32] Yet despite such momentary thaws, hopes for a Protestant Reformation never materialized. The missionaries ultimately created independent Protestant churches that were chiefly populated with converts drawn from the native churches.

A third characteristic key to understanding early mission work and its strategy was the internal debate and tension between civilizing and Christianizing. The missionaries wanted others to adopt their religious beliefs and practices and, at the same time, they wanted them to adopt Western political, educational, and societal norms. The latter desires were born out of earlier attempts to convert American Indians. Early Puritan missionaries to the American Indians strongly emphasized evangelism.[33] Yet they found it necessary to "civilize" the Indians; that is, to teach them colonial arts, sciences, and culture, in order to convert them. By the 1700s, the common view was summed up by Cotton Mather, the prominent Protestant preacher. "The best thing we can do for our Indians is to Anglicize them."[34] "They must be civilized ere they could be Christianized."[35] The missionaries thus considered education, democracy, health care, and economic growth to be complementing and tightly interwoven goals of missionary work.[36] As Samuel Hopkins explained, education was particularly important:

> For knowledge, mental light, and holiness are inseparably connected; and are, in some respects, the same. Holiness is true light and discerning, so far as it depends upon a right taste, and consists in it; and it is a thirst after every kind and degree of useful knowledge; and this desire and thirst for knowledge, will be great and strong, in proportion to the degree of holiness exercised... Therefore, a time of eminent holiness, must be a time of proportionally great light and knowledge.[37]

At its founding, the ABCFM adopted the twin goals of civilizing and Christianizing the world with a necessary priority placed on the first.[38] The balance between the two would shift back and forth over the years. When the ABCFM was created in 1812, Christianizing was its ultimate aim. Its declared purpose was "devising ways and means, and adopting and prosecuting measures, for the spread of the gospel in heathen lands."[39] Its laws and regulations called for the Board to "propagate the gospel among unevangelized nations and communities by means of preachers, catechists, school masters, and the press."[40]

Rufus Anderson, during his tenure as the ABCFM's secretary, heartily emphasized Christianizing and his five principles of mission work clearly center on evangelism:

1. The aim of the apostle was to save the souls of men.

2. The means he employed for this purpose were spiritual; namely, the gospel of Christ.

3. The power on which he relied to give efficacy to these means, was divine; namely, the promised aid of the Holy Spirit.

4. His success was chiefly in the middle and poorer classes,—the Christian influence ascending from thence.

5. When he had formed local churches, he did not hesitate to ordain presbyters over them, the best he could find; and then to throw upon the churches thus officered, the responsibilities of self-government, self-support, and self-propagation. His "presbyters in every church," whatever their number and other duties, had doubtless the pastoral care of the churches.[41]

The proper role of civilizing, in his view, was more complicated. In *Theory of Missions to the Heathen,* Anderson spoke of New England civilization as being the "highest and best, in a religious point of view, the world has ever seen." Yet at the same time, it was a "formidable hindrance" in evangelizing non-Christians because missionaries often expected converts to "come into all our fundamental ideas of morals, manners, political economy, social organization, right, justice, equality; although many of these are ideas which our own community has been ages in acquiring."[42] For Anderson, the solution was for missionaries to keep Christianizing as the primary goal. "Education, schools, the press, and whatever else goes to make up the working system, are held in strict subordination to the planting and building up of effective working churches."[43] Civilizing efforts were a means to that end. Education was necessary to cultivate independent churches and native pastors who would undertake the long-term goals of transforming society. "Without education, it is not possible for mission churches to be in any proper sense self-governed; not, without it, will they be self-supported, and much less self-propagating."[44] The ABCFM enshrined Anderson's ideas as official mission policy in 1856 despite objections from many who felt civilizing should have greater prominence.[45]

When Anderson left the ABCFM in 1866, the pendulum swung back towards civilizing. Educational efforts exploded after 1870 and by 1902, missionaries were operating more schools than churches.[46] The shift in emphasis was also related to the response of the native populations. New schools were welcomed far more than new churches, and the missionaries found it easier to recruit students than converts. Schools were a quick path to achieving tangible, quantifiable results.[47] Yet evangelism remained a foundational goal of the early missionaries.

A similar tension can be seen within the BFMPC. The 1861 Charter of the BFMPC declared the organization was created "for the purpose of establishing and conducting Christian missions among the unevangelized or pagan nations, and the general diffusion of Christianity."[48] Anderson's views heavily influenced Robert Speer, the long-serving head of the BFMPC and Speer did much to propagate Anderson's view within the missionary community. Like Anderson, Speer heavily emphasized Christianizing.[49] "The aim of foreign missions [is] to make Jesus Christ known to the world with a view to the full salvation of men, and their gathering into true and living churches." It is a "mischievous doctrine" to suggest that missions "must aim at the total reorganization of the whole social fabric."[50] At the same time, Speer did not see civilizing in a negative light, but rather as an intrinsic and inevitable consequence of evangelism. "There is a false imperialism which is abhorrent to Christianity, and there is a true imperialism which is inherent in it."[51]

The tension between the twin goals of civilizing and Christianizing would grow over the years, and Anderson's forceful focus on the latter anticipated the deeper divisions that would eventually emerge during the fundamentalist-modernist debates. In the same way that the fundamentalists and modernists would spar over the supernatural elements of traditional Christian theology (Biblical inerrancy, miracles, the deity of Christ, etc.) so the early missionaries would spar over whether to emphasize the supernatural benefits of Christian salvation or the secular benefits of schools and hospitals. For the time being, both sides forged a consensus that allowed a broad range of denominations to cooperate despite their differences. Congregationalists and Presbyterians, post-millennialists and pre-millennialists, liberals and conservatives could all support the twin goals for civilizing and Christianizing. The consensus guided American Protestant mission work for one hundred years.[52]

By the eve of World War I, the theological and strategic foundation for mission work had substantially changed. Two of its key pillars, millennialism and the civilizing-Christianizing consensus, were crumbling. Mainline missionaries began discarding beliefs in divine intervention, spiritual salvation and a literal millennial kingdom. Hope for societal progress remained, but it was centered on human efforts rather than divine will. "Belief in Christ's return on the cloud was superseded by the idea of God's kingdom in this world, which would be introduced step by step through successful labors in missionary endeavor abroad and through creating an egalitarian society at home."[53] The prevailing millennialism within the mainline churches, in other words, had removed "all supernatural features" that stressed the workings of the Spirit in favor of the more secular civilizing advancements of education, health, technology and democracy.[54]

Bosch identifies two broad factors behind the demise of "supernatural" millennialism. The first was a series of unmet millennial expectations leading up to World War I. William Miller, a Baptist layman, had predicted Christ would return to earth sometime between 1843 and 1844. He and his followers

gained notoriety as the date approached and when their
predictions failed to materialize, they divided internally and
outsiders derided them. Their failure cast doubt and aspersions
on millennial beliefs in general. Similarly, the Civil War
represented another millennial disappointment:

> Most 'mainline' Christians (the majority of whom were
> evangelicals) agreed that slavery was a scourge that had
> to be eradicated. Many were convinced that, once slavery
> was abolished, justice and equity would be the order of
> the day. The war turned out to be much more drawn out
> and much more brutal than either side had anticipated.
> Perhaps even worse—the end of the war did not usher in
> the expected utopia. People became aware that social
> problems had increased rather than decreased.[55]

The societal ills brought by industrialization and
urbanization also set-back post-millennial faith in science and
technology. Immigrants from Europe and rural America moved
to the cities for work and changed "the entire fabric of the
nation." The change confronted churches with new problems and
that contrasted with expectations of continual, upward progress.[56]

A second broad factor adding to unmet millennial hopes
was a theological shift towards "high criticism" of the Bible.
This approach treated the Bible as a historical document that
needed to be independently verified by other sources before it
could be accepted as fact. Many prophetic passages that were the
basis for millennial beliefs were called into question by scholars
using the high critical methods. As Bosch notes, the change had
major implications:

For the first time American theological schools were exposed on a large scale to the historical critical method in biblical studies, which had been dominant in German theological schools since at least a century before. Scholars now argued that the Bible did not propound only *one* "canonical" view on eschatology. And it was suggested that the books of Daniel and Revelation, long the mainstays of millennial speculations, were of later origin than had always been assumed and were therefore less reliable than had been thought... The inevitable victim of the new era was millennialism in any form, whether pre or post... it simply ebbed away.[57]

The shift towards "high-criticism" in the United States had deeper implications for the missions movement. It corresponded with the rise of "modernism," a philosophical and cultural perspective that sought to break with the past. Among mainline churches and especially the Congregationalists that formed the backbone of early missionary effort, the break was dramatic. Writing in 1915, James Barton, the Foreign Secretary of the ABCFM from 1892-1927, publically voiced views that would have been unthinkable thirty years before. He held that "modern" missionaries no longer believe unequivocally that all non-Christian religions are false. "The modern missionary goes out with the purpose of conserving all true values in the religious thought, life, and practices of the people whom he approaches."[58] Another key change identified by Barton was a shift in emphasis from individuals to society:

The missionary today is consciously face to face with the great national, social problems of the countries in which he is located... The successful solution of these problems will produce a religious as well as a social revolution for the non-Christian world.[59]

Yet the deepest and most dramatic change he noted was a secularized reinterpretation of Christian "salvation:"

> There is no doubt that one of the principal doctrines taught by the missionaries in the earlier part of the last century was the doctrine of salvation for the world to come... When a person was asked if he were "saved," it was implied to mean saved from eternal destruction and to eternal happiness. At the present time, the missionary preaches salvation no less than before, but it is salvation for the life that now is—salvation to oneself and for himself, and to society and for society—salvation for the sake of the world in which he lives. It is now taken for granted that if a man is saved for the life that now is, he will be abundantly prepared for the life that is to come. Our Lord announced that his mission upon earth was to give abundant life; the modern interpretation would say that Christ came to fit men to live and to live now. Missionaries today throughout the world are preaching to non-Christians the possibility through Christ of being saved now—saved from the sin of their present and past life, saved from evil habits, evil thoughts, evil purposes— saved from the destruction of their immortal life and made fit to live among men. Little emphasis is placed upon redemption in order that one may inherit an eternal life of rest and peace with God.[60]

Barton's views and those of the ABCFM did not reflect the sentiments of all mission organizations; Robert Speer of the BFMPC, for example, remained resolutely committed to evangelism. Yet Barton's views highlighted the movement's crumbling consensus on civilizing and Christianizing. When added to the changing views on millennialism, the movement's foundation was precariously brittle as it entered World War I; it was ill-prepared to weather the material and theological challenges the conflict would bring. As will be seen, the war and other aspects of international politics had a tremendous impact on mission work. Before discussing that impact, however, the influence of mission work on international politics will be covered.

Impact of Mission Work on International Politics

Missionaries influenced international politics directly through lobbying efforts and indirectly through the political consequences of their work. With respect to the first avenue, missionaries represented the American government's most important interest group within the region leading up to World War I.[61] American business interests in the Middle East were limited and oil was just beginning to be discovered. "The missionary lobby was one to be feared or respected by politicians, statesmen, and other policymakers even if the homage-payer did not agree fully with its sentiments."[62] Their views had a steadily growing influence on Middle East foreign policy that climaxed during the Wilson administration and the post-war peace talks. Missionary views were not monolithic, of course, and there were disagreements over goals and strategies. Nonetheless, the missionaries broadly advocated on behalf of the people groups they were connected to, including the Armenians,

Arabs, Bulgarians, and Assyrians. They also, unsurprisingly, advocated for their own protection and interests.

In addition to these direct lobbying efforts were the indirect consequences of their work. As will be seen, the indirect influence was ultimately much larger than the direct influence. The indirect influence of missions work also notably stemmed from efforts to civilize rather than Christianize the region. The schools founded by the missionaries cultivated Western values and views on government, society, and culture. The graduates of missionary schools would foster substantial political changes in their respective countries. Both direct and indirect means of influence will be analyzed on a case by case basis starting with the missionaries' attempts to protect their own interests and then moving on to consider the political impact they had on other people groups.

There are numerous examples of missionaries using their political clout to protect and extend their work within the region. In 1842, for example, Secretary of State Daniel Webster ordered the American ambassador to the Ottoman Empire to "omit no occasion… to extend all proper succor" to the missionaries there.[63] Theodore Roosevelt once considered sending U.S. warships to Turkey in response to the abduction of an American missionary.[64] Writing retrospectively, the ABCFM annual report of 1922 acknowledged, "For nearly a century, missionaries and their institutions have been protected by foreign powers."[65]

Likewise in the midst of World War I, the BFMPC praised the
U.S. ambassador to the Ottoman Empire Henry Morgenthau:

> Not only has he discharged his official duties in relation
> to our work with conspicuous fidelity, but he has also,
> with rare wisdom and tact, counseled with the
> missionaries, and used his personal influence in their
> behalf with the Turkish Government. We feel that it is in
> large measure due to him that the work of Missions has
> been permitted to go forward with comparatively little
> interference.[66]

In addition to protecting their own personnel and
property, the missionaries lobbied for the independence and self-
determination of many people groups in the region and indirectly
encouraged nationalist movements through their schools.
Nowhere was the missionary influence greater and nowhere did
the missionaries express stronger views than with regards to
Armenia. For one, missionaries were deeply invested in the
Armenian community. Missionary lobbying and "Christianizing"
led to the creation of a new Protestant Millet within the Ottoman
Empire that was chiefly populated by Armenian converts.[67] The
new Millet was, by definition, a political entity and one notably
distinct from the other Millets within the Empire. It was more
democratic in organization and benefitted from the schools and
hospitals built by the missionaries.[68] It thus offered a tantalizing
picture of the progress and reforms desired by many within the
Ottoman Empire regardless of their religion:

> Even if being *Prote* (Protestant) was regarded by many
> Muslims and non-Muslims as opprobrious, heretical, and
> subversive, both in the capital and the provinces,

modernity, freedom, and progress were broadly associated
by Muslims and non-Muslims alike with American
Protestant agency in the second half of the nineteenth
century. The positive image, particularly in the
countryside, was due to the missionary schools, hospitals,
and factories.[69]

The economic and political influence of the missionaries put
them at odds with the Ottoman government. "Protestantism as
represented by the ABCFM, which fundamentally called into
question the traditional Muslim cohesion and power, became a
main ideological enemy."[70]

The missionaries' response to persecution against
Armenians further politicized their relationship with the Turks.
Attacks began to intensify at the turn of the century. When they
occurred, missionaries called attention to them and James Barton
published a collection of first-hand missionary accounts of
violence. Public sympathy for the Armenian Christians led to
calls for U.S. intervention and one Protestant publication even
argued that Americans were obligated to respond to the crisis
because the missionaries had "stimulated the Armenian spirit of
independence" and the repressions were a reaction against it.[71] A
letter written to Woodrow Wilson from William Nesbit
Chambers, a Congregationalist missionary, provides an
illustrative example of missionary calls for intervention:

> The Armenian situation in Turkey is so appalling in its
> awful cruelty and relentless extermination of that people
> that one could wish that such a power as the United States
> should become so strong on land and sea that such a
> government as Turkey would never dare to commit such a

horrible crime. Would that your influence could be
exerted in some way to stay the spoiler and rescue the
miserable remnant.[72]

Chambers underscored his point by recounting an occasion when

he preached a sermon on an American warship:

> I stood with one hand on a great gun, and in the other was
> the Gospel—the one made for the destruction of men and
> the other revealed for their life and peace. I could satisfy
> myself only with the thought that the world needs them
> both. In the hands of such men as yourself the one would
> be used to restrain evil and the other to develop
> righteousness and good-will to men.[73]

Although the U.S. did not intervene, the American public became

very sympathetic to the idea of Armenian autonomy because of

the attacks. Following World War I, these sentiments would

heavily influence U.S. policy towards Turkey.

Of all the people groups in the Middle East, American

missionaries had the most complicated relationship with the

Turks. The Ottoman Empire was the most powerful political

entity within the Middle East and a pivotal player in international

relations. Most of the people groups the missionaries worked

with lived under Ottoman rule and Ottoman laws shaped

missionary policy by regulating how and where they operated.

Politically, the missionaries' views of Turkey varied

greatly over the years. At first, they saw the Ottoman Empire as

an obstacle to the restoration of a Jewish homeland in the Middle

East. As a political entity, the empire was thus to be opposed and

hopefully destroyed.[74] Beginning around 1830, attitudes changed as the missionary emphasis shifted from converting Jews and Muslims to revitalizing the indigenous Christian churches. Missionaries set aside restorationist ambitions for a Jewish state in favor of revivalist ones for Turkey; hopes for the destruction of the Ottoman Empire turned to hopes for its reform.[75] Their political views thus became more sympathetic and supportive. Missionary enthusiasm for Turkey peaked in 1908 when a collection of Turkish entities favoring reform rebelled against the Ottoman Sultan Abdul Hamid II. Known collectively as the Young Turks, many of their leaders had graduated from the missionary-run Bosphorus University and the revolution triggered euphoric hopes that the long-sought reform of the Empire were finally at hand.[76] The ABCFM's Missionary Herald hailed the "sudden conversion" of Turkey and the missionaries "followed a strongly pro-Ottoman policy" after 1908.[77] Hopes quickly soured. Favorable political views of the Young Turks waned as the latter became increasingly dictatorial and focused on a Turkish and Muslim national identity.[78] The 1913 *coup d'état* by the party, the abandonment of reforms in 1914, and the Ottoman entry in World War I on the side of the Germans particularly incensed the missionaries. However, even after these events, the missionaries heavily lobbied the U.S. to *not* declare war on Turkey because they feared a conflict would jeopardize their efforts and assets in the region. James Barton played a key role as the ABCFM publically proclaimed its position in the Missionary Herald. "Should the United States declare war against Turkey and Bulgaria? We say, unqualifiedly and emphatically, 'No.' It would be a tactical blunder, an outrage against humanity, and a moral crime."[79] Barton also enlisted the support of Cleveland Dodge, a friend of President Wilson with deep ties to the Middle Eastern missionary community. Dodge had served as the President of the Board of Bosphorus University and two of his children, Bayard and Elizabeth, were missionaries in the region. (Bayard would notably go on to serve as the President of AUB.)[80] Dodge, after receiving unanimous support from the Protestant Boards in the Ottoman Empire, wrote a personal letter to Wilson advocating neutrality towards Turkey in order to protect the mission work there.[81] The efforts of Barton, Dodge, and others ultimately prevailed and the U.S. did not declare war against the Ottomans.

During the war, waves of anti-Armenian violence erupted and the missionaries, who had close ties to the Armenian population, witnessed first-hand the genocidal attacks upon them. Many of the schools and churches the missionaries founded became depopulated as Armenians were killed or forcibly migrated. After the war, Barton called for a U.S. mandate and the ABCFM published a supportive editorial in the Missionary Herald. Other missionaries joined the call, including Caleb Gates, the President of Bosphorus University, and John Merrill, the President of the Central Turkey College. Barton hoped that an independent Armenian state would be partitioned from Turkey and that the presence of U.S. troops would guarantee its security.

(Gates notably did not support full independence because he felt it was not an ideal long-term solution.)[82] In the end, the Treaty of Sevres provided for an independent Armenian state, but the U.S. refused to accept a mandate. The Turkish nationalist revolt effectively annulled the treaty and the provisions never came into effect.

The missionaries played a role in negotiating and supporting the subsequent Treaty of Lausanne. Barton and the ABCFM lobbied the Harding administration to fully participate in the treaty conference, but the latter demurred and opted for only 'informal' representation. At the same time, it appointed Barton himself as an official advisor to the American delegation and representative of the various mission boards involved in the Middle East. Gates likewise served as an official advisor. At the conference, the American delegation again advocated for the creation of an independent Armenian state but this time to no avail. The British and French were unenthusiastic and President Harding offered only lukewarm support. The idea was eventually defeated by an adamant Turkish government that denounced the missionaries as troublemakers.[83]

The Treaty of Lausanne was unpopular among Americans in general and especially American Christians because it failed to provide for an independent Armenian state as had the earlier Treaty of Sevres. Nonetheless, missionaries publicly supported the treaty and urged others not to succumb to anti-Turkish rhetoric. In 1923 Barton wrote a letter to Henry Cabot Lodge,

Chairman of the Senate Foreign Relations Committee, expressing his support for the treaty and a hope that "in the discussion of the treaty a great deal of wild talk will not be indulged in against the Turk. The Turk is bad enough the Lord knows, but if we have to live with him and cooperate with him we gain nothing by constantly reminding him and others that he is a scoundrel."[84] Caleb Gates also publically supported the treaty.[85]

The efforts of Barton, Gates, and others provoked sharp rebukes from Christians within the United States. Barton lamented that "I have been tremendously criticized even in our own circle, for having been so conspicuous in promoting the treaty."[86] Gates likewise bemoaned that support for the Turk was for many "equivalent to eternal damnation."[87] Despite their controversial efforts, the Senate did not ratify the Treaty of Lausanne and it would take several more years before the U.S. and Turkey normalized relations.

Within the Ottoman Empire were a large number of Arabs and the relationship between them and the American missionaries provides yet more insight into the influence of mission work on international relations. The missionaries established a number of schools that were largely populated with Arab students including, most notably, the American University in Beirut (AUB) and the American University in Cairo (AUC). The American instructors sympathized with the political plight of their students and advocated for Arab self-determination.

Howard Bliss, the President of AUB and son of the
university's founder Daniel Bliss, offers a good example.
Following World War I, he traveled to the Paris Peace
Conference to lobby the Allies on behalf of the Arabs:[88]

> My plea before this body on behalf of the people of Syria
> is this: that an Inter-Allied or a Neutral Commission, or a
> Mixed Commission, be sent to Syria—including
> Lebanon—to express in a perfectly untrammeled way
> their political wishes and aspirations, viz: as to what form
> of government they desire and as to what Power, if any,
> should be their Mandatory Protecting Power.[89]

The Allies conceded to Bliss's request and President Wilson
established the King-Crane Commission to gauge public opinion
in the region. Many members of the Commission were
missionaries. Henry Churchill King, the commission's co-leader,
had himself just previously directed the YMCA's work in
France.[90] Charles Crane had served on the board of the
missionary-founded Bosphorus University.[91] The Commission's
concluding report declared that "in due time the Moslems will
prove themselves able to build up and manage their own states in
the Arabian and Anatolian peninsulas." The Entente powers
should "definitely and publicly renounce all further political
encroachments on that world, and outline a clear policy of
uplifting the Moslems."[92]

The lobbying efforts of missionaries had little long-term
impact, but the schools they founded had a much larger influence
on Middle-East politics by fomenting Arab nationalism. They
taught students Western ideas on politics, economics, science,

and society and offered an alternative to the Ottoman, multinational concept of the state. The students embraced this more secular, nationalistic view and the schools became centers of Arab nationalism. The AUB, for example, was the home of the first Arab nationalist organization. David Stuart Dodge, the AUB's President from 1996 to 1997 and great-great-grandnephew of Cleveland Dodge, explained the school's role in encouraging Arab nationalism. "The College fostered an atmosphere of free thought and free discussion which helped give birth to Arab nationalism, and allowed Arab nationalism to develop. You could almost say that Arab nationalism grew up out of the College."[93]

The AUC encouraged similar nationalist sentiments. Charles R. Watson, the university's founder, felt missionary efforts should become intertwined with Arab nationalism. "Nationalism marks a new stage in the life of a people and with it are born new impulses, new longings, and expectations, the spirit of inquiry and open-mindedness. Would it not be a thousand pities for the missionary enterprise to fail to avail itself of this new force in a country's life?"[94] So strong was the involvement of American missionaries in the rise of Arab nationalism, Robert Kaplan, an American journalist and expert in Middle Eastern affairs, attributes the political revolts in the region to their activities. "The Arab Revolt, which (T.E.) Lawrence wound up leading, was merely the military corollary to the American missionary-led Arab Awakening that took place in the cities of

Syria in the nineteenth century."[95] The initial Arab Revolt of
1916-1918 ultimately failed in the sense that the Gulf and Levant
continued to be controlled by foreign powers—Britain and
France merely replaced the oversight of the Ottomans. It would
eventually emerge victorious, however, with the subsequent wave
of revolts that swept the region following World War II.

      Missionary views towards the establishment of a Jewish
state offer a complex case study. As mentioned, the early
missionaries hoped to see a Jewish homeland restored within the
region. Pliny Fisk and Levi Parsons, the ABCFM's first two
missionaries to the Middle East, both strongly supported the
establishment of a Jewish homeland there. They were not alone.
Millennial theology held that Israel would be restored prior to the
second coming of Christ. J.T. Barclay, a Jerusalem-based
missionary, authored a lengthy work on the subject and predicted
the restored Jerusalem "will cover an area of more than a hundred
square miles; and will number its inhabitants by millions."[96]
Efforts to evangelize Jerusalem, however, bore little fruit, and, in
1843, the ABCFM decided to abandon its presence there.[97]

      In time, the missionaries became more sympathetic to the
Arab perspective. The King-Crane Commission opposed
restoring a Jewish homeland within the Middle East. "Jewish
immigration should be definitely limited, and that the project for
making Palestine distinctly a Jewish commonwealth should be
given up."[98] Two presidents of AUB, Howard Bliss and Bayard
Dodge, likewise opposed the creation of a Jewish state.[99] In a

1947 letter published in the New York Times, they opposed the
proposed U.N. partition plan. "Although many Arabic-speaking
peoples have no racial and little religious prejudice against the
Jews, they will undoubtedly rise up to defend what they believe
to be their rights if Palestine is divided."[100] The letter was co-
signed by Harold B. Hoskins, a diplomat born in Beirut to
missionary parents, Allen O. Whipple, a doctor born to
missionary parents in Urmia, and Albert W. Staub, a missionary
and Executive Director of Bosphorus University. In a 1948
essay, Dodge pointed out that "only in one part of the proposed
Jewish state do the Jews outnumber the Arabs" and the proposed
partition would put the Arabs at a severe economic disadvantage:

> It is the hills and mountains, generally speaking, that go to
> the Arabs and the fertile plains to the Jews. Palestine's
> only safe wintertime port—Haifa—will be in the Jewish
> State. The principle cash export of Palestine is citrus
> fruits. The citrus groves are owned approximately half
> and half by Arabs and Jews. Virtually all of them will be
> in the Jewish State. The Jewish State gets an
> overwhelming proportion of all the other economic values
> in Palestine… what is proposed is an Arab State which
> would start off as an international mendicant.[101]

Dodge, moreover, predicted the proposed partition would
provoke intense Arab opposition and dire consequences:

> All the work done by our philanthropic nonprofit
> American agencies in the Arab world—our Near East
> Foundation, our missions, our YMCA and YWCA, our
> Boston Jesuit College in Baghdad, our colleges in Cairo,
> Beirut, Damascus—would be threatened with complete
> frustration and collapse. So would our oil concessions…

> In place of economic development and stability, there will be confusion, left-wing control and a fertile opportunity for social revolution. What bigger chance could Russia want toward the accomplishment of its ancient and continuous ambition to reach down through the Middle East to "warm water" ports on the Persian Gulf? [102]

He also argued that it was unfair to force Arab nations to accept Jewish refugees and immigrants when the U.S. itself was unwilling to make similar accommodations. "Can we really contend that the Arabs have a duty to be more hospitable to refugees than we are?"[103]

The AUC provides another interesting example of anti-Zionist sentiments. In 1945, a group of AUC professors lobbied against a Congressional resolution calling for the U.S. to aid in the establishment of a Jewish state. In 1946, the University's president, John Badeau, warned President Truman of the danger of basing U.S. policy on "internal American politics"—a reference to lobbying efforts by Jewish-American groups. Following Truman's recognition of Israel in 1948, Badeau cabled a lengthy protest calling the move "unjust to Palestinian Arab rights and prejudicial to the best interests of the United States in the Middle East."[104]

The missionaries' relationship with Arab Christians partially explained their political views. The missionary schools were generally populated with Arab Christians who were opposed to the creation of a Jewish state.[105] George Wadsworth, the American Consul-General (and a former AUB professor) noted that the Arabs influenced Christian missionaries and both shared concerns over Jewish "domination" of the region and immigration.[106]

The pro-Arab sympathies of American missionaries contrasted sharply with many of the movement's supporters in the U.S. William Blackstone, a successful Chicago businessman and fervent financial contributor to mission organizations, authored a petition in 1891 (the "Blackstone Memorial") that called on the U.S. government to support politically the creation of a Jewish state.[107] Over 400 public figures signed the petition, including many well-known Christian clergymen. Following World War I, Blackstone led the Presbyterian General Assembly into passing a resolution in support of a Jewish homeland.[108] This was at a time when the AUB's Howard Bliss was calling for the Allies to grant Arabs political self-determination—a move that would have knowingly prevented the creation of a Jewish state.[109] Similarly, after World War II when Dodge and Badeau were warning of the dire consequences of partitioning Palestine, Reinhold Niebuhr and Paul Tillich, leading Protestant theologians of the day, were lobbying in favor of a Jewish state through the Christian Council on Palestine.[110]

While missionaries at AUC and AUB were encouraging Arab nationalism, their counterparts at Bosphorus University were encouraging Bulgarian nationalism. Writing in 1909, George Washburn, a Congregationalist minister and the University's president from 1877 to 1903, described the role that the college and he himself played in encouraging Bulgarian

Independence:

> The College is best known in Europe for the influence that it had in building up a free state in the Balkan Peninsula... The most important thing that we ever did for them was the educating of their young men to become leaders of their people at a time when there were very few Bulgarians who knew anything of civil government in a free state
>
> This was our legitimate work and naturally and inevitably led to our doing what we could for them after they left the College to give them the advice which they sought in their new work and to defend their interests where we had influence in Europe. That in this way we had an important part in the building up of this new state is a fact known to all the world and best of all by the Bulgarians themselves who have never failed to recognize their obligation to the College and to manifest their affection for us as individuals.[111]

Bulgaria gained de facto independence in 1908 and for his role in the process, Washburn was hailed as the "Father of Bulgaria" and decorated by the King of Bulgaria in recognition. His successor, Caleb Gates, was similarly decorated for supporting Bulgaria.[112]

Iran presents yet another case of American missionary influence. The U.S. government appointed its first ambassador to Iran, S. G. W. Benjamin, at the request of an American missionary in Iran, and Benjamin himself was the son of missionaries working in Turkey.[113] For two decades, the protection and wellbeing of the BFMPC missions was the primary concern of U.S. policy towards Iran.[114] When revolution

erupted in 1906, a young American working for the BFMPC,
Howard C. Baskerville, joined the revolutionaries and later died
in combat becoming an Iranian national hero.[115] He was not the
last missionary to die in conflict there.

During World War I, Iran, although officially neutral,
became a theater of war between Russian, British, and Ottoman
troops. The Ottomans twice attacked and occupied Urmia, the
seat of American mission efforts to the nation. During the first
occupation in 1915, Kurdish irregulars looted, raped, and
massacred the city's population.[116] American missionaries tried
to remain neutral while protecting and succoring Assyrian and
Armenian Christians. Disease spread throughout the city killing
3,000 of the 15,000 people under missionary care including the
wife of William Shedd, the head of the mission station.[117] By the
time of the second attack in 1918, the U.S. had declared war on
Germany (but not the Ottoman Empire) and the missionaries
were decidedly supporting the Entente side of the conflict.
Shedd, a long-time friend of BFMPC head Robert Speer, was
also serving as the U.S. Vice-Console in Urmia and was helping
to organize the city's defenses. His efforts occurred against the
express wishes of the U.S. government. He coordinated with the
British Army as part of the effort and even supplied money, arms,
and munitions for the Armenian and Assyrian troops that had
been mobilized to fight the Ottomans.[118] Another missionary,
Harry Packard, organized the city's police force. Shedd defended
his and Packard's actions, claiming:

...that the safety of the whole community and the possibility of doing relief work at all depended on the defeat of the Turkish attempt to take this place and that we were not only justified in aiding the Syrian and Armenian military forces but were compelled to do so. Accordingly we have done so and the amount of help given is large amounting to forty or fifty thousand dollars. We have reason to believe that this will be refunded by the British Military authorizes, although we have no guarantee that this will be the case.[119]

Despite their efforts, the city fell to the Ottomans again and the city's Christian population fled in fear. Shedd accompanied the refugees and died of cholera in the process. The American missionaries that remained in Urmia, including Packard, were briefly interned by the Ottomans and then released after the war.[120]

The actions of the missionaries during the war tarnished their image among Iranian Muslims. William Shedd would later be referred to as "one of the leaders of the Christian community, who supplied and armed them and incited them to fight the Muslims."[121] In 1919, Harry Packard attempted to return to Urmia and a riot broke out in response. "In some ways it was the result of a growing popular Iranian perception that Americans were associated with Assyrian and Kurdish attacks on Iranian Muslims."[122] The riot ended the Presbyterian presence in Urmia until 1923. At that time, Packard was still not allowed to return to the city. The Iranian Foreign Minister Mohammad Mosaddeq claimed, "Dr. Packard has been involved in the revolutionary movements… his return to Urmia may renew the past difficulties."[123]

In the wake of the conflict, the ABCFM helped establish a "Persian Commission" backed by the U.S. Department of State and led by Harry Pratt Judson, president of the University of Chicago. The Commission provided relief to the Assyrian refugees and lobbied the U.S. to assume a League of Nation's mandate there. The BFMPC's Robert Speer likewise called on President Wilson to provide "full security" for the Assyrian Christians in Iran.[124] Their calls for a mandate went unheeded, however, and Britain became the key foreign power in Iran following World War I.

Examining the missionaries' political influence on the Armenians, Turks, Arabs, Jews, Bulgarians and Assyrians reveals two consistent patterns. Firstly, attempts at direct lobbying usually bore little fruit. Calls for Arab self determination and a U.S. mandate over Assyrians went unheeded. Protests against the establishment of a Jewish state in the region were overlooked. The chief successes of lobbying efforts were the United States' decision to *not* declare war on Turkey and the inclusion of an independent, Armenian state within the Treaty of Sevres. Yet the treaty provisions did not last long. Ataturk's successful rebellion against the Ottoman Sultan abrogated the treaty and similar provisions were not obtained in the subsequent Treaty of Lausanne. Missionaries calls for an Armenian mandate were dismissed the second time around.

Secondly, the indirect influence of the missionaries was much greater than the direct influence. The schools established by the missionaries did much to encourage nationalist movements among the Bulgarians, Arabs, Armenians, and Turks. Many of these movements were successful and all had strong political implications for the region. Bulgaria established autonomous authority from the Ottoman Empire in 1878 and formal independence in 1908; the Young Turk movement weakened the Sultan's power and paved the way for the Republic of Turkey after World War I. Arab nationalist movements eventually rose to power over the British and the French following World War II.

With the influence of mission work on international politics now assessed, we will turn attention to the influence of international politics on mission work. As will be seen, the reverse influence was much stronger. International politics had a dramatic and enduring impact on the American missions movement.

Impact of International Politics on Mission Work

One of the ways missionaries felt international politics was impacting their work was through the perceptions it created about Christians and Christianity. The ABCFM's James Barton articulated a fairly developed understanding of how this was occurring in the Middle East during the first wave of missionary work. Despite his modernist views, James Barton strongly believed Christians needed to convert Muslims. Prior to becoming the Foreign Secretary of the ABCFM, Barton was a missionary in Turkey and then president of Euphrates College in Harput. He wrote a book, *The Christian Approach to Islam,* dedicated to the subject of Christian witness to Muslims, and his views offer an interesting argument of how international politics influences mission work. In Barton's view, the reason Muslims had not already adopted Christianity, despite years of efforts, related to the inadequacy of the Christian witness. Christians within the region were making Christianity unappealing by the way they behaved personally:

> From the day of its inception until the beginning of the
> last century, Mohammedanism never came into close,
> continuous contact with a pure Christianity. Its very
> beginning was a protest against a Christianity that, in its
> worship, had all the appearance, at least, of idolatry. The
> Mohammedan leaders then, as well as in subsequent
> generations, saw nothing in Christians which made them
> believe that Christianity could be better than their own
> religion. The Christianity with which Islam was in
> conflict was not such a manifestation in the lives and
> practices of its followers as to compel the intellectual
> approval of Moslems or even to command their attention.
> All the churches of Syria, Armenia, and Asia Minor had
> become worldly and formal, from which had departed the
> gentle spirit of their Lord, who exalted meekness, truth,
> purity, and righteousness.[125]

Missionaries to the region were making lionhearted efforts, in his view, but had to confront centuries of damage caused by contact with "impure" Christianity. Western Christians outside the region were also to blame for making Christianity unappealing through their political behavior:

We need not refer back to the conflict beginning even in the days of Mohammed and extending all down through the centuries, but to the more recent contacts of Mohammedans in Turkey, for instance, with the Armenian, Greek and Syrian races, which have from the beginning been more or less in conflict with the Mohammedan government, — and it must be confessed that in multitudes of instances they have not revealed the true spirit of Christ in dealing with their Mohammedan neighbors. Turkey has repeatedly complained of her treatment at the hands of Russia, a so-called Christian country, and it must be confessed that Russia's dealings with Turkey have not all been along Christian lines. The same may be said of the Christian nations of Europe, who have exploited Turkey and have used, in this exploitation, their great military strength and power. The result has been that the Mohammedans of the Turkish empire, and undoubtedly, through them, the Mohammedans of other countries, have been greatly influenced; they have looked upon Christianity as a hostile religion, believing that a nation that has become Christian will necessarily be opposed to any Mohammedan country, this fact being emphasized by the gradual elimination of Mohammedan nations and peoples as independent governments, and the setting up over them of Christian rule. It is natural that the Mohammedans of North Africa, Arabia, Egypt, the entire Turkish Empire, and Persia, should regard Christianity as a religion of oppression that sets itself up as the enemy of Mohammedanism and the subjugator of Mohammedan countries.[126]

Barton felt the political relationship between Christian nations and Muslim nations was "perhaps the greatest difficulty" in winning converts to Christianity.[127] Missionary efforts were going to be hamstrung until the Western nations changed their politics.

Setting aside Barton's concerns of the religious impact of political policies, it is clear that international political events had a strong impact on mission work in the region. To begin with, World War I dramatically setback mission efforts to the Middle East. "That foreign missionaries and their operations are seriously and fundamentally affected all will agree."[128] Numerous factors afflicted mission work. For one, the war disrupted communications between the missions and their home offices in America and drew potential missionary recruits to the front lines. This not only cut off the flow of information from the mission stations but also the flow of money, supplies, and personnel.

Secondly, the war dramatically increased the cost of supplies and travel, which put tremendous financial strain on missionary organizations. Barton described the challenges:

> The financial loss of the missions has been great, caused by the increased cost of nearly all commodities everywhere. No part of the world is free from the apparently universal advance in the price of foodstuffs, labor, and of wearing apparel. This has compelled the increase of the annual allowance for the support of missionaries. At the same time, the cost of transportation, both of the missionary and his supplies, has more than doubled, and to this is to be added the increase of cost of exchange, brought about chiefly by the rise in the price of silver.[129]

War, epidemics, and famines took their toll. The flood of Armenian and other refugees spread disease across the region. About five percent of the missionaries who remained in the region during the conflict died, mostly due to typhus, typhoid, and cholera.[130]

Warfare and the Turkish army also halted mission work. Most of the churches, schools, and hospitals in Turkey were closed, destroyed, or appropriated by the government. The ABCFM annual report of 1918 described the impact:

> In short, of all the 151 American missionaries in the field and of all the great work which was in full progress in 1914, but 36 missionaries were left in the field in 1918, while churches, schools and hospitals, with the exception of those at Constantinople and Smyrna, have practically been closed or wiped out of existence.[131]

The war dealt a similar blow to the BFMPC's mission in Urmia, Iran. Ottoman and Kurdish incursions into the city dramatically reduced Urmia's Christian population and nearly wiped out a century of mission work there. Urmia was "reduced to a desert, and the American schools and hospitals there were completely destroyed."[132] Of the thirty ordained men serving churches in Urmia, only two remained after the war.[133] The BFMPC Annual report summarized the situation saying, "We face an apparently complete wreck of the efforts of the last 80 years."[134] The war also dramatically heightened religious tensions there between Christians and Muslims by pitting Ottoman and Kurdish Muslims against Russian, British, Armenian, and Assyrian Christians. In 1917, a violent conflict erupted between Muslims and Christians after the Assyrian religious leader, Mar Shimoun, was assassinated by Kurds.

Assyrian Christians responded by massacring and looting Muslims in Urmia for several days.[135]   Across the region as a whole, 75% to 85% of the missionaries were compelled to abandon their posts because of the war.[136]

Following World War I, mission organizations hoped to rebuild their presence in the region. Although the war had wrought havoc on their work, they saw a spiritual opportunity within its political consequences. The BFMPC claimed that "it will be many years before the full effects of the war, upon the Mohammedanism, can be known, but there can be no doubt that the door of present opportunity is wider than it has even been."[137] The ABCFM perceived a similar opportunity and explained its cause:

> Reports coming from different parts of the entire area occupied speak of a marked change in the attitude of the Mohammedans toward Americans and towards Christianity. This is due in part, unquestionably, to the disrupted state of Mohammedanism as represented in Turkey. Confidence has been lost in the Caliph of Islam, who is now in the hands of the Allies in Constantinople, and a realizing sense that Mohammedanism hardly seems destined to become a dominate militant religion. On the other hand, these people have seen what Christianity is doing for the saving of life and ameliorating the sad condition of the various populations in Turkey, and it is not surprising that the Mohammedans and the Kurds should be usually friendly towards Americans and the message which they bring. There is an increasing number of inquirers, and not a few outstanding conversions among them.[138]

The post-war political upheavals dashed these hopes. The ABCFM Annual Report of 1922 describes a "year of horrors" for mission work in Turkey. The 1920 Kemalist revolt against the sultan abrogated the Treaty of Sevres. The renegotiated Treaty of Lausanne stripped the missionaries of the foreign power protection. As the ABCFM explained, "The effect of the abolition of the Capitulations upon our work has been deep. It has demanded a complete readjustment in the thinking of those engaged in missionary work in Turkey."[139]

The new government commanded the missionaries to stop evangelistic efforts. Many of the mission stations were permanently abandoned. Moreover, the Kemalists sought to "Turkify" the nation and expel religious minorities. This uprooted the Christians living within Turkey and with them, the communities long associated with the missionaries. In the end, the ACBFM greatly reduced its presence in Turkey and shifted its efforts from evangelism to educational and humanitarian work.

Added to the political and military challenges brought by the war were the genocidal campaigns against the Armenian civilians living in Turkey. At the turn of the century, anti-Armenian violence swept the Ottoman Empire. The first wave occurred from 1894-1896 and resulted in the death of 100,000 to 300,000 people.[140] A second wave, concentrated in the southwest province of Adana, occurred in 1909 and resulted in the death of 10,000 to 30,000 people. These attacks culminated in wider genocidal campaigns conducted from 1915 to 1923.[141]

The American missionaries energetically responded. James Barton and Cleveland Dodge formed a relief organization that would eventually raise and distribute $100 million worth of food, clothing, and temporary shelter to the Armenians.[142] They likewise called public attention to the massacres through articles, speeches, and by publishing a volume of eye-witness accounts.

Despite the missionaries' relief efforts "the Armenian population of Anatolia and historic West Armenia was eliminated."[143] Those that survived the genocidal campaign were forced to migrate elsewhere. Barton described the brutal impact on the Armenians and American mission work:

> This attack upon the Armenians, who comprised the larger part of the student and teaching force and working Christian body in Asiatic Turkey, struck a direct blow at the educational and missionary work. Native professors in American colleges, teachers, pastors, leaders, and students in the educational institutions were seized by the thousands, some of them horribly tortured, many put to death, while others were sent into exile down into Syria and northern Arabia….The effect upon educational work in the interior of Turkey was paralyzing, as in the College at Aintab, Euphrates College at Harput, and the College at Van. Nearly every Armenian teacher was at once eliminated and the older students either taken into the army, exiled, or killed.[144]

The elimination of the Armenian people in eastern Turkey meant the elimination of a century of American mission work there. ABCFM annual reports speak of Protestant communities being "practically wiped out." Churches were seized; seminaries were forced to suspend operations.[145] ABCFM statistics illustrate the devastating impact of these events on mission efforts to

Turkey. The number of missionaries, churches, and converts

plummeted. The mission to eastern Turkey was completely

eliminated during World War I and the subsequent Armenian

genocide (see Table 2).[146]

Table 2 ABCFM missionary statistics for the Middle East, 1912 vs. 1924.

Indicator	1912	1924	Change in Number	Change in Percent
American ordained preachers	38	32	-6	-14%
Total American missionaries	160	138	-22	-13%
Native ordained preachers	83	16	-67	-79%
Total native workers	1,164	286	-878	-81%
Churches	132	27	-105	-83%
Congregants	14,317	2,515	-1,1802	-85%

Sources: ABCFM, *1913 Annual Report*, (Boston: ABCFM, 1913), 95.
ABCFM, *1924 Annual Report*, (Boston: ABCFM, 1924), 3.
Note: Totals exclude the Balkans.

Even after the conflict ended, effects lingered. The

Turkish government required American missionaries to remain

silent about the events as a condition of operating in the country.

This posed a moral dilemma for the missionaries who, on the one

hand, were outraged at the atrocities but, on the other hand,

wished to continue their work. The ABCFM was internally

divided and in the end decided to comply.[147] The forced silence took a notable toll on missionary morale and was difficult for many to accept.[148]

World War I had a powerful impact on the American religious landscape and, in turn, mission work. The sight of Christian nations engaged in brutal, trench warfare contrasted with the secularized, post-millennial optimism that was infused into mainline Protestant beliefs. Moreover, the sight of "Christian" nations at war challenged the hitherto unquestioned superiority of Western civilization. The doubts were summed up by the question, "Has Christianity failed?" Writing in 1916, Barton argued that the war's impact on religion was greater than its impact on politics:

> No political changes however great and startling can equal in significance those that the war is bringing about in the realm of religion....We all distinctly recall the question that was heard upon every side when the war had been thoroughly launched and we began to realize its significance: Has Christianity failed? This was asked not only in countries not Christian and by those who were no friends of Christianity, but in the very citadels and historic centers of the Christian church and by those who for decades had been conspicuous Christian leaders. Christian and non-Christian, believers in Christianity and its opponents, suggested, by inquiry, the failure of Christianity because it did not prevent the conflict.[149]

The SVM quadrennial conference of 1919 was another key indicator of how deeply these doubts had spread. Long a source of recruits, the SVM's conventions brought together missionary-minded youth from across America and Canada. The aim of each conference was to call students to missionary service.

At the 1919 convention, however, SVM leaders were on the defensive and forced to make the case for Christianity. Speaking from the stage, Robert Speer disregarded prepared remarks and acknowledged the convention's doubts:

> There are things being said in this convention today, there are thoughts in our minds, and desires in our hearts, expressed and unexpressed in group after group which we will do well right here in the middle of this convention, and before we go, unhesitatingly, unflinchingly, to face and see through to the end. I am not going to say anything more about the worth or failure of non-Christian faiths. I am going to open quite candidly the question that some of you have been discussing right here in these days as to whether there is worth enough in our Christian faith…There are men here in this Conference, and women too, who are saying that Christianity here in America, and as expressed by this Student Volunteer Conference, is a failure…
>
> Are these saying true? Has the Christian religion failed? Are we failing Him? No, it has not failed. Christianity just as it is in Canada and in the United States today, imperfect, incomplete, discredited by the weakness of men, is the richest and purest and greatest power that there is in the world. The religion that we have got, short as it falls of all that Christ meant us to have, is worth carrying to all the world…
>
> No, Jesus hasn't failed, and He isn't going to fail, but I will tell you men and women that there is a danger of failure here tonight… that we ourselves may fail.[150]

Despite Speer's impassioned pleas, doubts continued to deepen and spread within the SVM. One observer to its 1924 conference noted, "There was not any expression of conviction on the part of the students that the way of Jesus is the way."[151]

A key point of contention between the students and the SVM's leadership was the war. The leaders, despite pacifist hesitations, had strongly supported the war and were heavily invested in the conflict, both emotionally and spiritually.[152] Robert Speer, for example, had declared, "The war was the greatest proclamation of foreign missions which we have ever heard."[153] When the harsh realities of war and its aftermath became apparent, students questioned the Christianity that had so strongly implored them into battle. "The church's countenancing of the war brought Christianity, and, by association, the missions movement, under attack by disillusioned and increasingly cynical students."[154]

The disillusionment that followed the war was not limited to students but pervasive among rank-and-file parishioners. The war dealt a near death-blow to Social Gospel theology which had become widely adopted among the mainline churches; faith in unrelenting progress could no longer be held. As Bosch notes, "The First World War and the malaise that followed it shattered to pieces the confidence that was an indisputable ingredient of the Social Gospel movement."[155] Robert T. Handy, a longtime church historian at Union Theological Seminary, similarly noted the widespread impact of the war:

> Protestantism was deeply affected by the general disillusionment of the postwar decade. During the war itself, the American people, with the vigorous support of most religious leaders, maintained a spirit of high optimism. But the tide turned swiftly....The rapid subsidence of the war spirit...led "to a wave of spiritual

depression and religious skepticism, widespread and devastating."[156]

While the war led many rank-and-file into deep spiritual doubt, it prompted many mission leaders to change and politicize the goals of mission work. Ironically, the same Social Gospel theology which was being abandoned by the rank-and-file was used as the basis for a renewed call for missions. "The war hastened the redefinition of evangelization. To respond to the war, the gospel had to have a more social content."[157] Mission leaders were pressed to explain how Christian nations could engage in war against each other and they began to recast salvation as a public social transformation rather than a private spiritual transformation. In this way, the salvation of society offered a permanent solution to the problems of war and poverty. James Barton again provides an illustrative example of the changing emphasis:

> In a word, the war has caused the world to recognize that Christianity is a religion that has a national and international mission and that it will not come to its own and accomplish its purpose until it puts the stamp of brotherhood upon the national life of the entire world. The war has discovered to us and the world our failure hitherto to grasp the national mission of our religion…

> The effect of the war upon Christianity is to bring to the front the fact that in Christianity there exists a moral and religious force capable of cementing the nations into a mighty brotherhood into which no unholy ambition for conquest or unholy race prejudice shall be permitted to disturb permanent order and lasting peace.[158]

The expanded, politicized goals vocalized by mission leaders had little chance of success given the doubts of the laity. With the theological rug pulled out from under the movement, enthusiasm for mission work dissipated. Hans-Lukas Kieser, a historian with expertise in both Ottoman history and Protestant theology, points out, "After 1918, there was no more missionary America in the sense of the century before; no more confidence and commitment for a postmillennialist mission, a Jesus-centered building up of modern institutions and civil society." "During and after World War I, belief in the force of faith and the nonviolent coming of the millennium seriously suffered, and the postmillennialist American mirror of history broke."[159] The celebrated missionary Pearl S. Buck similarly described the war's impact on mission work:

> From this hour the disintegration of missions began, because the impulse itself was shaken, the old divine belief gone. The mad years that followed the war, the economic readjustment, the desperate longing for refuge in pleasure, the selfishness of the individual search for such refuge, the lack of idealism in the young, both of those disillusioned in the war and of the generation immediately after, all had their inevitable results upon the missionary movement.[160]

The consequences of the theological earthquake could be seen across many dimensions of mission work. Students, long the source of missionary recruits, were now unenthusiastic about serving.[161] The ACBFM lamented, "Definite decisions for such service were comparatively few. Almost without exception, the colleges were found to be in the midst of the after-the-war reaction." The board also noted a changing attitude among the students. "Students freely admitted in interviews that their main thought was to find a career in which they could make money."

This experience foreshadowed a decline in recruits. In 1920, 2,700 students offered themselves for foreign mission work but, by 1928, that figure had dwindled to just 252.[162] The declining number of recruits further eroded the missionary ranks. The ABCFM missionary force, for example, peaked between 1922 and 1924 with roughly 820 missionaries world-wide, but by 1927 it had declined to just 762.[163] The BFMPC similarly hit its peak in 1926 with 1,606 missionaries worldwide.[164]

Mission agencies also began struggling financially. Costs from the war had driven both the ABCFM and the BFMPC into debt. In its 1920 report the ABCFM stated, "Difficult problems have confronted us on every side; at times they have seemed overwhelming"[165] The BFMPC likewise spoke of "grave financial anxieties."[166] Short-term financial challenges were eventually overcome but, by 1924 the ABCFM was bemoaning, "The showing in respect to the gifts of the churches has been grievously disappointing."[167] Financial contributions from churches, in similar fashion to the number of missionaries in the field, peaked in 1928 and then began to decline.[168] The board's experience, again, was not unique. Within five years of the war's end, fund-raising drives for missions in general were falling below expectations; 1921 proved to be the overall peak for financial contributions during this period.[169] A study by the United Stewardship Council noted an almost 40% decline in benevolence between 1921 and 1929.[170] These declines contrasted sharply with the rapid growth in contributions prior to World War I.[171] The ABCFM annual report of 1924 attributed the financial woes to a post-war decline in enthusiasm for mission work and issued a lengthy challenge to its supporting churches:

> In the opinion of your committee the time has come when we should urge upon the pastors and leaders of our churches the importance of engaging in a fresh and earnest study of the foreign missionary enterprise as it relates itself to the needs of the modern world and to the welfare of the church at home. As a friend of the Board recently put it, "There is a call to re-think this whole foreign missionary business..." During the past ten years, we have been occupied for the most part in endeavoring to overtake the financial situation arising from the Great War, whereby the cost of the work had increased approximately 75%... There can be no question of the ability of our churches to meet the demand of this as of all other lines of missionary effort. In the economy of God opportunity and capacity go hand in hand. Congregationalists do not lack the means to support their mission board. The situation appears to be that the few have given generously, the many have given in pitiable amounts, or not at all. Moreover, let it be known, it has been a period of unusual expansion in the matter of home equipment. Church edifices costing unheard of amounts, commodious parish-houses, new organs, elegant stained-glass windows are in evidence on every side. We have witnessed a noteworthy development in the staffing of the home church. In the more prosperous parishes, pastors' assistants, education directors, social service experts, are the order of the day. All this, we recognize, is a sign of

life and progress. We offer no word of censure, only of congratulation—provided there is no diminution in missionary vision and endeavor. We tremble for the church that lengthens her cords and strengthens her stakes at the expense of the men and women she sends into the sacrifice of the foreign field.[172]

Despite similar exhortations from other missionary leaders, contributions continued to sag and domestic church projects held priority over foreign missions.[173] The Great Depression "threw the whole Protestant missionary enterprise in reverse."[174] Contributions and the number of missionaries serving overseas dramatically declined. Yet the problem was not merely financial. As Robert Handy noted, "Even after the disastrous effects of the economic depression had overtaken the mission boards, there was clear recognition that the problem was much more than financial, and that it had predated the economic crisis."[175] Speer complained about the dearth of funds for mission work and blamed it on low enthusiasm more than financial inability. "The tobacco bill of the Church would do it alone, not to speak of the movies and the automobiles."[176]

By the 1930s, the first wave of American missionary effort had collapsed amidst theological turmoil. The modernist-fundamentalist debates erupted into the mission field with the 1932 publication of *Re-Thinking Missions: A Laymen's Inquiry After One Hundred Years.*[177] John D. Rockefeller Jr., heir to the Rockefeller fortune and long-time contributor to mission organizations, was concerned about the flagging enthusiasm for mission work and funded the multi-volume study as a means to reassess the movement and recommend a course of action. The final report heavily criticized mission work and spoke of "the necessity that the modern mission make a positive effort, first of all to know and understand the religions around it, then to recognize and associate itself with whatever kindred elements there are in them. The Christian will therefore regard himself a co-worker."[178]

Such pluralistic, syncretistic language further dismantled the pre-war theological consensus on civilizing and Christianizing. A majority of church lay members still held conservative theological views, but the mission leadership was divided between liberals who espoused the revised evangelism of the Hocking Report and moderates seeking to find middle ground.[179] Publication of the report and the wider modernist-fundamentalist debates pushed mission boards to plot a new theological course. Robert Speer and the BFMPC attempted to hold a moderate position. Speer heavily criticized the report, but there were internal divisions within the board. As early as 1922, the BFMPC felt compelled to require all of its missionaries to sign a statement agreeing that "Foreign Mission work is carried on to make our Lord Jesus Christ known to all men as their Divine Savior."[180] Speer's criticisms of the Hocking Report, moreover, did not go far enough for fundamentalists like G. Gresham Machen, a former professor at Princeton Seminary who had left the school to form a new, more conservative seminary in

1929. Machen strongly condemned the BFMPC's reaction and became a constant critic of the organization's theological doctrine. The BFMPC was also shaken by the lavish praise heaped on the Hocking Report by Pearl Buck, the Pulitzer and Nobel Prize winning wife of a BFMPC missionary to China. Divisions within the BFMPC eventually led to a split and the creation of a much smaller yet conservative and independent board.[181] The BFMPC continued its decline and, by 1942, was fielding 1,134 missionaries world-wide, a 29% drop from its 1926 peak.[182] Annual contributions to the board similarly declined almost 50% between 1924 (the peak year) and 1941.[183] By 1958, what remained of the BFMPC became part of the Commission on Ecumenical Mission and Relations within the United Presbyterian Church in the U.S.A., the forerunner to the Presbyterian Church (U.S.A.) which is today the largest Presbyterian denomination in the U.S., with over two million members. In 2011, the PCUSA General Assembly Mission Council fielded roughly 200 missionaries—little more than one-tenth the number fielded by the BFMPC at its peak. Of these, 14 were located in the Middle East as compared to the 133 missionaries present there under the BFMPC in 1922.[184]

The ABCFM responded to the theological controversy by resoundingly choosing a modernist path. It hailed the wisdom of the Hocking Report, and its secretary Hugh Vernon White declared, "The Christian mission should be a man-centered enterprise" and, "The service of man as the regulative aim of

Christian missions."[185] Copies of the Hocking Report were sent
to all of the ACBFM's mission stations.[186] Such actions,
however, alienated conservatives. One of its seminary graduates
in the Middle East lamented the changes:

> I cannot help but wonder what St. Paul and the dedicated
> missionaries after him would say about the work of our
> contemporary American Board of Foreign Missions that
> supports schools which forbid the mention of Jesus Christ
> and teach the Gospel of Mammon and Materialism.
> What, in fact, would the early founders of the American
> missions say about today's Board, which joins our
> politicians and businessmen in defense of those who
> justify or deny the Genocide and ongoing minority
> persecutions, lest the truth jeopardize business
> opportunities, covering all beneath the veil of "national
> security."[187]

The ABCFM missionary force rapidly declined from its
1922 peak of roughly 820 to 372 by 1942—a 54% decline. [188]
The organization's income from churches dropped 60% between
1928 and 1939.[189] It never recovered. By 1960, it was still
fielding only 363 missionaries—a figure comparable to 1942.[190]
In 1961 it merged with the Board of International Missions to
form the United Church Board for World Ministries. In 1995,
operations were combined with the Division of Overseas
Ministries of the Christian Church (Disciples of Christ) to form
Global Ministries—an entity that fielded just 54 missionaries
world-wide in 2011. Of these, 7 were located within the Middle-
East, a tiny figure compared to the 138 missionaries the ABCFM
had in the region in 1924.[191]

The SVM, for its part, had already undergone division

and a modernist makeover prior to the publication of the Hocking

Report. At the 1927 convention, Sherwood Eddy, a longtime

leader within the SVM, acknowledged that the current generation

of students no longer sought, "The evangelization of the world in

this generation."[192] In 1928, the Moody Bible Institute withdrew

from the SVM because of its increasingly liberal outlook.[193] The

move had tragic symbolism because the SVM had been born out

of student meetings led by D.L. Moody, the founder and

namesake of the Moody Bible Institute. By the end of the 1930s,

the SVM was a shadow of its former self, employing only 4

people at its New York City headquarters (down from a peak of

29). Likewise in 1938 it procured only 25 volunteers, down from

nearly 3,000 in 1920.[194] It eventually merged with the United

Student Christian Council and the Interseminary Committee in

1959 to form the National Student Christian Federation (NSCF).

In 1966, the legacy entity within the NSCF, the Commission on

World Missions, was disbanded.[195]

The decline of the SVM, ABCFM, and BFMPC

underscores the direct and indirect influence international politics

can have on mission work. World War I presented many

practical challenges to the missions movement including

increased expenses, the interruption and destruction of mission

work, and a limited ability to transport materials, personnel, and

information to and from the field. The war also had a

tremendous, indirect impact on the missions movement by raising questions and increasing internal tensions. The pre-war consensus that had guided the movement for over a century eventually broke apart under the strain and when it did, efforts ground down to a halt.

Summary

The first wave of American Protestant missionary effort was deeply intertwined with the international relations of the Middle East. The missionaries had a measure of influence on international relations. The schools founded by American missionaries played a key role in the nationalist movements that swept the region both before and after World War I. The missionaries also politically supported these movements by lobbying, at the highest levels, for the creation of independent Arab and Armenian states by way of a U.S. mandate in the region. The results of direct lobbying efforts were lackluster, however. The U.S. refused to assume a mandate and the French and British took control over Arab lands—no independent states were formed until after World War II. The missionaries did succeed in providing for an independent Armenian state within the Treaty of Sevres (a high-water mark of their influence), but the Kemalist revolt ultimately annulled the provisions. Missionary objections to the establishment of a Jewish state did little to slow the birth of Israel. It is also notable that the missionaries' influence on international relations generally grew from efforts to civilize the region rather than efforts to Christianize it.

The impact of international relations on mission work was much greater than the influence of the latter on the former. International events alternatively opened and closed the door to mission work. Great Britain's strong regional influence and protection increased the missionaries' access to the Middle East as did American naval power after the turn of the century. World War I, on the other hand, greatly reduced their access and wiped out a century of mission work in Western Iran; anti-Armenian violence similarly destroyed work in eastern Turkey.

International relations also had indirect consequences on mission work. The disillusionment that followed World War I greatly undermined American enthusiasm for mission work and brought the first wave of effort to an end. The missionaries themselves also perceived opportunities and challenges inherent in political events—James Barton saw colonialism as a negative witness to Christianity; others felt the abolition of the Ottoman Caliphate would increase doubts about the veracity of Islam.

In conclusion, an analysis of the first wave of American Protestant missionary work illustrates the complicated, bi-directional influence between international relations and mission work. American missionaries during this time were not simply agents of imperialism—they often advocated on behalf of people groups in the region. American missionaries were also affected by their missionary experiences and international politics.

Desires for an independent Jewish state in the region gradually transformed into opposition. Enthusiasm for mission work waned with the disillusionment of war. American Protestant missionaries and the international politics of the Middle East influenced each other in deep, lasting ways, and the political lobbing of missionaries was one of the least consequential influences within this dynamic. Having analyzed the relationship between historical mission work in the Middle East and international politics, I will now present an analysis of contemporary, second wave mission efforts and its underlying theology.

---

1 Gerald H Anderson, "American Protestants in Pursuit of Mission: 1886-1986," International Bulletin of Missionary Research 12, no. 3 (July 1988): 105. The American Board of Commissioners for Foreign Missions (ABCFM) and the Board of Foreign Missions of the Presbyterian Church (BFMPC) used minor variations in naming conventions for their annual reports. In order to clarify source citation, all citations simply refer to the "ABCFM Annual Report" or "BFMPC Annual Report" for the appropriate year; ABCFM, 1924 Annual Report, (Boston: ABCFM, 1924), 3; BFMPC, 1922 Annual Report, (New York: BFMPC, 1922), 372, 378, 436.

2 Thomas Cole Richards, *The Haystack Prayer Meeting: An Account of its Origin and Spirit* (Boston: The Haystack Centennial Committee, 1906), 16-17, 22.

3 Ibid; Gerald H. Anderson, *Biographical Dictionary of Christian Missions* (Grand Rapids: William B. Eerdmans Publishing Company, 1998), 460; Global Ministries, "The History of the Haystack Prayer Meeting," http://www.globalministries.org /resources/mission-study/what-is-haystack/the-history-of-the-haystack-pray.html (accessed August 12, 2011).

4 David W. Kling "The New Divinity and the Origins of the American Board of Commissioners for Foreign Missions," *Church History 27*, no. 4 (December 2003).

5 William R. Hutchison, *Errand to the World: American Protestant Thought and Foreign Missions* (Chicago: University of Chicago Press, 1993), 45, 95.

[6] Ian Tyrrell, *Reforming the World: The Creation of America's Moral Empire* (Princeton University Press, 2010), 51.

[7] Ibid., 51, 62.

[8] Hutchison, *Errand to the World*, 1.

[9] Ibid., 91.

[10] Anderson, "American Protestants," 101.

[11] Tyrrell, *Reforming the World*, 67.

[12] Ibid; Hutchison, *Errand to the World*, 93.

[13] Ibid., 91.

[14] Edward Earle Mead, "American Missions in the Near East," *Foreign Affairs 7*, no. 3 (April 1929): 405-406, 409-410, 417.

[15] Michael B. Oren, *Power, Faith, and Fantasy: America in the Middle East, 1776 to the Present Day* (New York: Norton & Company, 2007), 127-128.

[16] Ibid., 128.

[17] Gordon Taylor, *Fever & Thirst: A Missionary Doctor Among the Tribes of Kurdistan* (Chicago: Academy Chicago Publishers, 2005), 109-110.

[18] ABCFM, *1916 Annual Report* (Boston: ABCFM, 1916), 112.

[19] At the time, Iran was known as Iran. (The official name of the country was changed in 1935.) For simplicity's sake I consistently use "Iran."; BFMPC, *1914 Annual Report* (New York: BFMPC, 1914), 334, 348, 447.

[20] John DeNovo, *American Interests and Policies in the Middle East: 1900-1939* (Minneapolis: The University of Minnesota Press, 1963), 9-10; Note: By common consent, the key missionary boards agreed to geographically divide their activities.

[21] Ibid; ABCFM, *1916 Annual Report*, 112; BFMPC, *1914 Annual Report*, 334, 348, 447.

[22] Bosch, *Transforming Mission*, 314.

[23] Oren, *Power, Faith, and Fantasy*, 88.

[24] Note: Not all of the missionaries were post-millennialists. D. L. Moody is a good example of a pre-millennialist that enthusiastically supported the missions movement.

[25] Kieser, *Nearest East*, 44.

[26] Pikkert, "Protestant Missionaries," 69-70.

[27] Rufus Anderson, *History of the Missions of the American Board of Commissioners for Foreign Missions to the Oriental Churches*, Vol. 1 (Boston: Congregational Publishing Society, 1872), 1-2.

[28] Ussama Makdisi, *Artillery of Heaven: American Missionaries and the Failed Conversion of the Middle East* (Ithaca: Cornell University Press. 2008).

[29] Badr, "American Protestant Missionary Beginning," 217-227.

[30] Oren, *Power, Faith and Fantasy*, 120.

[31] H. G. O. Dwight, *Christianity in Turkey a Narrative of the Protestant Reformation in the Armenian Church* (London: James Nisbet & Co., 1854), 215-216.

[32] Makdisi, *Artillery of Heaven*, 168.

[33] Hutchison, *Errand to the World*, 24.

[34] Ibid., 29.

[35] Makdisi, *Artillery of Heaven*, 26.

[36] Joseph L. Grabill, *Protestant Diplomacy and the Near East: Missionary Influence on American Policy*, 1810-1927 (Minneapolis: University of Minnesota Press, 1971), 5.

[37] Ernest Lee Tuveson, *Redeemer Nation: The Idea of America's Millennial Role* (Chicago: The University of Chicago Press, 1968), 60.

[38] Pikkert, "Protestant Missionaries," 47-48; Hutchison, Errand to the World, 65.

[39] ABCFM, *Memorial Volume of the First Fifty Years of the American Board of Commissioners for Foreign Missions* (Boston: ABCFM, 1861), 405.

[40] Ibid., 79.

[41] Rufus Anderson, *Foreign Missions: Their Relations and Claims* (New York: Charles Scribner and Company, 1869), 109-110.

[42] Rufus. Anderson, "The Theory of Missions to the Heathen," in *The American National Preacher. Volume 20,* ed. W. H. Bidwell (New York: W. H. Bidwell, 1845), 180.

[43] Anderson, *Foreign Missions,* 113-114.

[44] Ibid.

[45] Gerald Anderson, *Biographical Dictionary of Christian Missions*, 20; Cemal Yetkiner, "At the Center of the Debate: Bebek Seminary and the Education Policy of the American Board of Commissioners for Foreign Missions (1840-1860)," in *American Missionaries and the Middle East: Foundation Encounters,* ed. Mehmet Ali Doğan and Heather J. Sharkey (Salt Lake City: University of Utah Press, 2011).

[46] Hutchison, *Errand to the World*, 100.

[47] Ibid., 98.

[48] BFMPC, *1914 Annual Report.*

[49] R. Pierce. Beaver, "The Legacy of Rufus Anderson," *Occasional Bulletin of Missionary Research 3*, no. 3 (July 1979).

[50] Anderson, "American Protestants in Pursuit of Mission," 101.

[51] Hutchison, *Errand to the World*, 91.

[52] Ibid., 95.

[53] Bosch, *Transforming Mission*, 321.

[54] Ibid.

[55] Ibid., 320.

[56] Ibid.

[57] Ibid., 320-321.

[58] James L. Barton, "The Modern Missionary," *Harvard Theological Review* 8 no. 1 (January 1915): 4.

[59] Ibid., 7.

[60] Ibid., 15-16.

[61] DeNovo, *American Interests*, 8.

[62] Tyrrell, *Reforming the World*, 191.

[63] Oren, *Power, Faith and Fantasy*, 121.

[64] Ibid., 311.

[65] ABCFM, *1923 Annual Report* (Boston: ACBFM, 1923), 51.

[66] BFMPC, *1916 Annual Report* (New York: BFMPC, 1916), 13-14.

[67] The Ottoman "Millet System" established separate, autonomous jurisdictions for each confessional community.

[68] Kieser, *Nearest East*, 48-49.

[69] Ibid., 49.

[70] Ibid., 56.

[71] Tyrrell, *Reforming the World*, 104.

[72] William Nesbit Chambers to Wilson, December 10, 1915 in *The Papers of Woodrow Wilson, v35 October 1, 1915 – January 27, 1916*, ed. Arthur S. Link (Princeton: Princeton University Press, 1981), 337.

[73] Ibid.

[74] Kieser, *Nearest East*, 39.

[75] Ibid., 44-47.

[76] Oren, *Power, Faith, and Fantasy*, 326.

[77] Kieser, *Nearest East*, 67, 92.

[78] Ibid., 76-80.

[79] Grabill, *Protestant Diplomacy*, 94.

[80] Ibid., 88-89.

[81] Ibid., 92.

[82] Ibid., 169-172.

[83] Ibid., 269-272.

[84] Ibid., 276.

[85] Ibid., 283.

[86] Ibid., 284.

[87] Ibid., 276.

[88] "University Challenge: The Future," *The National* (May 8 2009), http://www.thenational.ae /article/20090509/FOREIGN/705089824/1011/FOREIGN (accessed September 17, 2011).

[89] "In Our History: Negotiating Peacetime," *Main Gain: The American University of Beirut Quarterly Magazine 5*, no. 3 (Spring 2007), http://staff.aub.edu.lb/~webmgate/spring2007/article9.htm (accessed September 17, 2011).

[90] Kieser, *Nearest East,* 108.

[91] Ussama Samir Makdisi, *Faith Misplaced: The Broken Promise of U.S.-Arab Relations: 1820-2001*, New York: PublicAffairs, 2010, 139.

[92] "King-Crane report on the Near East," in *Editor & publisher* (New York: Editor & Publisher Co., 1922), Sec. III (Recommendations), III, III, II, (3).

[93] Kaplan, *The Arabists*, 37.

[94] Pikkert, "Protestant Missionaries," 171.

[95] Kaplan, *The Arabists*, 62.

[96] J.T. Barclay, *The City of the Great King: Jerusalem As It Was, As It Is, and As It Is to Be* (Philadelphia: James Challen and Sons, 1858), 613.

[97] A.L. Tibawi, *American Interests in Syria, 1800-1901* (Oxford: Clarendon Press, 1966), 105.

[98] "King-Crane report on the Near East," Sec. III (Recommendations), E. (Zionism), (3).

[99] Grabill, *Protestant Diplomacy*, 178.

Kaplan, *The Arabists,* 79-80.

[100] Daniel Bliss, et. al., "Against Palestine Partition," *The New York Times* (November 21, 1947): 26.

[101] Bayard Dodge, "Must There be War in the Middle East," *Reader's Digest 52*, no. 312 (April 1948): 38.

[102] Ibid., 40-41.

[103] Ibid., 45.

[104] Lawrence R. Murphy, *The American University in Cairo, 1919-1987* (Cairo: The American University in Cairo Press, 1987), 109-110.

[105] Oren, *Power, Faith, and Fantasy*, 368.

[106] Denovo, *American Interests*, 344.

[107] Anderson, *Biographical Dictionary*, 68.

[108] Paul Charles Merkley, *The Politics of Christian Zionism, 1891-1948* (London: Frank Cass Publishers, 1998), 68-69.

[109] Grabill. *Protestant Diplomacy*, 178.

[110] Merkley, *Politics of Christian Zionism*, 141-145.

[111] George Washburn, *Fifty years in Constantinople and recollections of Robert College* (Boston: Houghton Mifflin Company, 1909), 289-299.

[112] Grabill, *Protestant Diplomacy*, 54.

[113] The missionary's brother was a congressman from Ohio.

[114] Grabill, *Protestant Diplomacy*, 137.

[115] Baskerville applied to be a missionary as an undergraduate at Princeton University with a letter of recommendation from his history professor, Woodrow Wilson. Baskerville latter led 150 men in the defense of Tabriz, the seat of the Iranian Constitutionalists, and is still honored to this day in Iran. In 2005, Iranian President Mohammad Khatami dedicated a bust of Baskerville in Tabriz's Constitution House. Yellow roses are also anonymously left at his gravesite in the city; Farnaz Calafi, Ali Dadpay, and Pouyan Mashayekh, "Iran's Yankee Hero," *The New York Times* (April 18, 2009): A23; Michael Zirinsky, "American Presbyterian Missionaries at Urmia During the Great War," *Proceedings of the International Roundtable on Persia and the Great War*, Tehran, 2-3 March 1997

[116] Zirinsky, "Great War," 8.

[117] Ibid., 13.

[118] Grabill, *Protestant Diplomacy*, 140-143; Zirinsky, "Great War," 14-15.

[119] Notably, the British government did eventually refund the money, see Ibid., 15.

[120] Ibid., 10.

[121] Ahmad Mansoori, "American Missionaries in Iran, 1834-1934." (Ph.D. diss., Ball State University, 1986), 59.

[122] Zirinsky, "Great War," 11.

[123] Michael Zirinsky, "Render Therefore Unto Caesar the Things Which Are Caesar's: American Presbyterian Educators and Reza Shah," *Iranian Studies* 26.3/4 (Summer – Autumn 1993): 341.

[124] Grabill, *Protestant Diplomacy*, 146-151.

[125] James L. Barton, *Daybreak in Turkey* (Boston: The Pilgrim Press, 1908), 113.

[126] James L. Barton, *The Christian Approach to Islam* (Boston: The Pilgrim Press, 1918), 227-228.

[127] Ibid., 271.

[128] James L. Barton, "The Effect of War on Protestant Missions," *The Harvard Theological Review 12*, no. 1 (January 1919): 1.

[129] Ibid., 5-6.

[130] Ibid., 3-4.

[131] ABCFM, *1918 Annual Report* (Boston: ABCFM, 1918), 107.

[132] Zirinsky, "Render Therefore Unto Caesar," 340.

[133] John, Elder. *History of the Iran Mission* (New York: Literature Committee of the Church Council of Iran, 1960), 77.

[134] BFMPC *1920 Annual Report* (New York: BFMPC, 1920), 323.

[135] Zirinsky, "Great War," 9; Mansoori, "American Missionaries," 59-60.

[136] Barton, "Effect of War," 3.

[137] BFMPC, *1919 Annual Report,* (New York: BFMPC, 1919), 48.

[138] ABCFM, *1919 Annual Report,* (Boston: ABCFM, 1919), 38-39.

[139] ABCFM, *1923 Annual Report,* (Boston: ABCFM, 1923), 52.

[140] Rouben Paul Adalian "The Armenian Genocide," in *Century of Genocide 3rd. Edition,* ed. Samuel Totten and William S. Parsons (New York: Routledge, 2009), 70.

[141] Note: The exact death toll has been the subject of much debate. Estimates range from 200,000 to 2,000,000.

[142] In today's dollars, the amount would be the equivalent of $1 billion; Oren, Power, Faith, and Fantasy, 336.

[143] Adalian, "The Armenian Genocide," 55.

[144] Barton, "Effect of War," 10.

[145] ABCFM, *1919 Annual Report*, 85-88.

[146] The 1923 Annual Report for the ABCFM reported no churches or communicants within its eastern Turkey mission. This contrasts with 51 churches present in 1914 and 3,080 communicants; ABCFM, 1916 Annual Report, 112; ABCFM, 1923 Annual Report, 3.

[147] Kieser, *Nearest East,* 110.

[148] Ibid., 101.

[149] James L. Barton, "Reaction of the War upon Islam," *The Journal of Race Development 7*, no. 2 (October 1916): 187.

[150] Robert Speer, "The Personal Worth or Failure of Christianity," in *North American Students and World Advance,* ed. Burton St. John (New York: SVM, 1920), 176-179.

[151] Nathan D. Showalter, *The End of a Crusade: The Student Volunteer Movement for Foreign Missions and the Great War* (Lanham: Scarecrow Press, 1997), 110.

[152] Richard M. Gamble, *The War for Righteousness: Progressive Christianity, the Great War, and the Rise of the Messianic Nation* (Wilmington: ISI Books, 2003), 178-179, 207-208.

[153] Showalter, *End of a Crusade*, 22.

[154] Ibid., 90-91.

[155] Bosch, *Transforming Mission*, 326.

[156] Robert T. Handy, "The American Religious Depression, 1925-1935," *Church History 29*, no. 1 (March 1960): 6.

[157] Ibid., 52; Gambel, *Protestant Diplomacy*, 252.

[158] Barton, "Reaction of War upon Islam," 187.

[159] Kieser, *Nearest East,* 98, 116.

[160] James Allan Patterson, "Robert E. Speer and the Crisis of the American Protestant Missionary Movement, 1920-1937" (Ph.D. diss., Princeton Theological Seminary, 1980), 65.

[161] Barton, "Effect of War," 4.

[162] Handy, "The American Religious Depression," 4.

[163] ABCFM, *1942 Annual Report,* (Boston: ABCFM, 1942), 55.

[164] Anderson, "American Protestants," 108.

[165] ABCFM, *1920 Annual Report,* (Boston: ABCFM, 1920), 13.

[166] BFMPC, *1919 Annual Report,* 1.

[167] ABCFM, *1924 Annual Report,* 23.

[168] ABCFM, *1939 Annual Report,* (Boston: ABCFM, 1939), 32.

[169] Tyrell, Reforming the World, 227; Anderson, "American Protestants," 105.

[170] Handy, "The American Religious Depression," 4.

[171] Anderson, "American Protestants," 105.

[172] ABCFM, *1924 Annual Report*, 27-29.

[173] Patterson, "Robert E. Speer," 70.

[174] Anderson, "American Protestants," 107.

[175] Handy, "The American Religious Depression," 4.

[176] Patterson, "Robert E. Speer," 85.

[177] The report was also commonly referred to as the "Hocking Report" after the name of the committee chairman, William Hocking.

[178] The Commission of Appraisal, *Re-Thinking Missions: A Laymen's Inquiry After One Hundred Years* (New York: Harper & Brothers Publishers, 1932), 33.

[179] Archibald G. Baker, "Reactions to the Laymen's Report," *The Journal of Religion 13*, no. 4 (October 1933): 398; Hutchison, Errand to the World, 165.

[180] BFMPC, *1922 Annual Report*, 12.

[181] Hutchison, *Errand to the World*, 174.

[182] Anderson, "American Protestants," 108.

[183] BFMPC, *1941 Annual Report*, (New York: BFMPC, 1941), 170.

[184] PCUSA General Assembly Mission Council, e-mail message to author, Dallas, August 20, 2011.

[185] Anderson, "American Protestants," 107.

[186] Patterson, "Robert E. Speer," 96.

[187] Kieser, *Nearest East*, 126.

[188] ABCFM, *1942 Annual Report*, (Boston: ABCFM, 1942), 55.

[189] ABCFM, *1932 Annual Report*, 32.

[190] ABCFM, *1960 Annual Report*, (Boston: ABCFM, 1960), 109.

[191] Global Ministries, e-mail message to author, August 22, 2011.

[192] G. Sherwood Eddy, "Can we still believe in foreign missions?" in *Students and the Future of Christian Missions*, ed. Gordon Poteat (New York: SVM, 1928), 78-79.

[193] Showalter, *End of a Crusade*, 158-159.

[194] Ibid., 161, 180.

[195] Ibid., 181-182.

Chapter 2: Contemporary Missions

The American missions movement substantially changed
after World War I. In the Middle East, the war interrupted and in
places it destroyed mission work that was established over nearly
a century. The "religious depression" of the 1920s and
fundamentalist-modernist controversies divided the missions
movement and depleted it of funds, personnel, and vitality. The
economic depression of the 1930s further undermined the
movement's finances.[1] World War II, like World War I, forced
many mission organizations to halt their efforts. In sum, the
inter-war period was one of great decline for the American
missions movement.

Despite these set-backs, the number of American
missionaries began to increase again after World War II and
quickly surpassed its previous peak. In 1952, there were 18,599
North American Protestant missionaries working overseas—an
increase of roughly 4,000 over the 1925 peak.[2] By 1956, the
number had swelled 25% to 23,432; the number continued to
grow over the following decades, reaching 50,002 in 2008. Even
after adjusting for population growth, there has been a marked

increase in the number of North American missionaries. In 1925, there were approximately 12 missionaries for every 100,000 people in North America (the bulk of which was from the United States.) In 1952, there were just 11 missionaries per 100,000 pop, but by 1956 the number had risen to 13 per 100,000 pop. The 2008 number was even greater: 15 missionaries for every 100,000 pop and, in the United States, the average was 15.5 missionaries for every 100,000 pop.[3] The growth was impressive but missionary statistics alone do not convey the profound changes that occurred within the movement during the inter-war period.

The second wave of mission effort was not a resurgence of the churches and organizations that had directed the movement prior to World War I. As noted above, the last vestiges of the Student Volunteer Movement (SVM) were disbanded in 1966. The ABCFM , once the largest player in the American missions movement, dwindled to become a very minor player. The BFMPC weathered the inter-war period better but substantially declined nonetheless; today (as part of the Presbyterian Church U.S.A.) it fields roughly 200 missionaries or one-tenth the number fielded prior to World War I.[4] The decline of these three key organizations mirrors the decline among mainline churches in general. As mission historian Gerald Anderson notes, "Main-line boards began to rebuild after a twenty-year period of decline and disruption, but they would never fully recover."[5] The second wave of American mission work was a new movement more than resurgence; a new beginning rather than a continuation.

The mission boards that dominated the first wave period were affiliated with mainline Protestant churches and their representative association, the National Council of Churches (NCC). Many of the boards that eventually displaced the dominant, fist-wave organizations broke from mainline organizations prior to 1930. The modernist-fundamentalists doctrinal disputes were a chief cause of division. For example in 1917, a collection of fundamentalist organizations formed the Interdenominational Foreign Mission Association (IFMA). Among them were the Africa Inland Mission, the Central American Mission (now CAM International), the China Inland Mission (now Overseas Missionary Fellowship International), the South Africa General Mission and Sudan Interior Mission (now united as Serving In Mission). All of these organizations play a significant role in the missions movement today. Similarly in 1927, the American Baptist Missionary Union reprimanded one of its missionaries, Raphael Thomas, for openly advocating evangelism over humanitarian work.[6] Thomas subsequently resigned and founded the Association of Baptists for World Missions (ABWG) which today fields nearly 800 missionaries.[7] Other factors besides doctrine caused splits. The Southern Baptist Convention broke from the Northern Baptists in 1845 over the issue of slavery and subsequently became one of the largest players in the missions movement fielding over 5,000

missionaries in 2010.[8] Assemblies of God World Missions
(AGWM) grew out of the Pentecostal movement in 1914 and
became another major mission organization, fielding over 2,200
missionaries.[9]

The dominate first-wave boards were also displaced by
new, non-denominational boards formed outside of the NCC after
World War II. Campus Crusade for Christ, for example, was
established in 1951 and fields nearly 1,300 missionaries along
with over 12,000 national workers.[10] It sees itself, in part, as the
modern-day conservative successor to the Student Volunteer
Movement:

> In 1948, The Student Volunteer Movement splintered, its
> evangelistic core feeling increasingly unwelcome joined
> with a newly formed college ministry and held their first
> missions conference in Urbana, Illinois. The group is
> known as InterVarsity and was soon joined by Campus
> Crusade for Christ and other campus ministries: a whole
> new missionary enterprise once again springing from the
> campus and flowing out to the world.[11]

Other organizations founded during and shortly after
World War II achieved similar levels of success. New Tribes
Mission (established in 1942) fields 922 missionaries.[12] Partners
International (established in 1943 as The China Native
Evangelistic Crusade) supports 4,278 national workers.[13] World
Vision (established in 1953) is one of the largest, Christian,
humanitarian, organizations in the world with over 40,000
employees and $1 billion in revenues.[14]

Aside from the organizational legacy of the mission boards, the second wave of mission effort distinguishes itself from the first wave in several respects. For one, it is less concentrated, organizationally speaking. The five largest mission boards active during the first wave of effort accounted for 43% of mission expenditure (see Table 3).[15]

Table 3 Largest Mission Organizations by Income (1911)

Organization	Headquarters	Income ($1,000s)	Income as % of Total
American Board of Commissioners for Foreign Missions (ABCFM)	Boston, MA	$1,092	9%
Board of Foreign Missions of the Presbyterian Church (BFMPC)	New York, NY	$1,314	11%
American Baptist Missionary Union	Boston, MA	$713	6%
Board of Foreign Missions of the Methodist Episcopal Church	New York, NY	$1,357	11%
Board of Missions of the Methodist Episcopal Church, South	Nashville, TN	$767	6%
Total -Top Five Organizations		$5,243	43%
Total -All Organizations		$12,122	100%

Source: James S. Dennis, et. al. *Word Atlas of Christian Missions,* New York: Student Volunteer Movement, 1911.

Conversely, the five largest, second-wave organizations, in terms of funding, account for just 27% of mission expenditure (see Table 4); the five largest in terms of missionaries account for 24% of all missionaries (see Table 5).

Table 4 Largest Mission Organizations by Income (2001)

Organization	Headquarters	Income ($1,000s)	Income as % of Total
World Vision	Federal Way, WA	$358,703	10%
International Mission Board of the Southern Baptist Convention (IMB)	Richmond, VA	$197,866	5%
Assemblies of God World Missions (AGWM)	Springfield, MO	$177,262	5%
MAP International	Brunswick, GA	$151,751	4%
Christian Aid	Berlin, OH	$132,988	4%
Total -Top Five Organizations		$1,018,570	27%
Total -All Organizations		$3,752,306	100%

Source: Dotsey Welliver and Minnette Northcut, *Mission Handbook 2004-2006: U.S. and Canadian Protestant Ministries Overseas,* Wheaton: EMIS, 2004.

A second difference between the first and second waves of mission work is the geographical center of the movement. The second wave of mission effort is centered in the Southern and Western United States; the first wave effort was centered in the Northeast United States. Almost all of the top five mission boards active during the first wave of effort were headquartered in New York or Boston (see Table 3). None of the top, second wave boards is headquartered in the Northeast United States (see Table 4 & Table 5).

A third difference between the two waves is the degree of centralization; the second wave of effort is less centralized than the first. During the first wave of effort, mission organizations directly supported missionaries as if they were employees.

Table 5 Largest Mission Organizations by Number of Missionaries (2001)

Organization	Headquarters	Missionaries	Missionaries as % of Total
International Mission Board of the Southern Baptist Convention (IMB)	Richmond, VA	5,437	12%
Assemblies of God World Missions (AGWM)	Springfield, MO	1,708	4%
New Tribes Missions	Sanford, FL	1,496	3%
Campus Crusade for Christ	Orlando, FL	1,096	2%
Baptist International Missions, Inc. (BIMI)	Chattanooga, TN	1,040	2%
Total -Top Five Organizations		10,777	24%
Total -All Organizations		44,386	100%

Source: Dotsey Welliver and Minnette Northcut, *Mission Handbook 2004-2006: U.S. and Canadian Protestant Ministries Overseas,* Wheaton: EMIS, 2004.

Today, the "faith-mission" model is common and with this model, missionaries raise funds from friends, family, and churches. Mission agencies, on the other hand, chiefly provide organizational structure and do not financially support their missionaries.

A fourth difference is found in the organization's focus and range of activities. First wave organizations sought to comprehensively transform foreign nations by establishing schools, hospitals, and churches. It was admittedly a long-term goal requiring effort on multiple fronts. Independent commissions oversaw short-term relief efforts. Second wave organizations, conversely, have a narrower focus. Most organizations either concentrate on inherently religious goals (church planting, evangelism, pastoral training) or humanitarian efforts (relief and development assistance), but not both. The establishment of schools and hospitals has become less important to mission efforts since World War I.

A fifth difference between the two waves is the role of government funding. Government financing of mission organizations dates back to the founding of the U.S. and it rapidly accelerated after World War II. The practice began when the U.S. used missionaries to establish diplomatic, cultural, and religious ties with American Indians.[16] For example in 1789, President George Washington and Henry Knox, the Secretary of War, pressed American Indians to accept a missionary presence among their tribes. Similarly, Presidents James Madison and

Thomas Jefferson advocated the use of government funds to support missionaries working among American Indians. Between 1819 and 1873, mission organizations received government financial support to establish and operate schools for American Indians.[17]

Although the government and mission organizations partnered to "civilize" American Indians, their relationship was at times tense and fraught with conflicts. Secretary Knox stipulated that "no attempt should be made to teach the peculiar doctrines of revealed religion except to those Indians to whom any of its mysteries have already been unfolded." Mission organizations resented restrictions on evangelistic efforts and the two parties also clashed over Indian policy. During the Andrew Jackson Presidency, the U.S. government began forcefully removing the Indian tribes from their land. The ABCFM vehemently opposed the policy and some of its missionaries were jailed by the state of Georgia for their resistance. The ABCFM brought the matter before the Supreme Court which ruled in its favor and ordered the release of the missionaries.[18]

During World War I, mission organizations and the U.S. government partnered to provide relief efforts. Herbert Hoover, at the time responsible for coordinating food aid to Europe, channeled government assistance through the American Friends Service Committee—a Quaker relief organization.[19] Following World War II this partnership greatly expanded. President Franklin Roosevelt and Secretary of State Cordell Hull expressly sought to regulate private charities and use them to distribute government funds. Roosevelt created a variety of government agencies to accomplish this goal and by the end of the war government funds for relief and refugee work were routinely flowing through religious organizations. By one estimate, 90% of post-war relief was being provided through religious agencies.[20]

The partnership forged during World War II continues today and government funds are routinely distributed through Christian humanitarian organizations which are, to varying degrees, evangelistic in their outlook and intent. These organizations raise private funds to complement government contracts but, in some cases, the latter comprise the lion's share of their program expenditures. For example, government grants constitute 63% of program expenses for World Relief, the relief and development arm of the National Association of Evangelicals (see Figure 1). Regulations forbid the use of government funds for expressly religious activities—a policy that can be traced back to Henry Knox's attempts to restrain evangelism efforts to American Indians.[21]

A final contrast between the first wave and second wave of mission effort is theology. Second wave organizations are theologically more conservative. Most of the organizations grew out of the fundamentalist or evangelical movements and hold to the "fundamentals" of Christianity.[22] They gradually displaced the mainline boards that by the end of the first wave period had

become theologically liberal.[23]

Government Grants Received by Select Christian

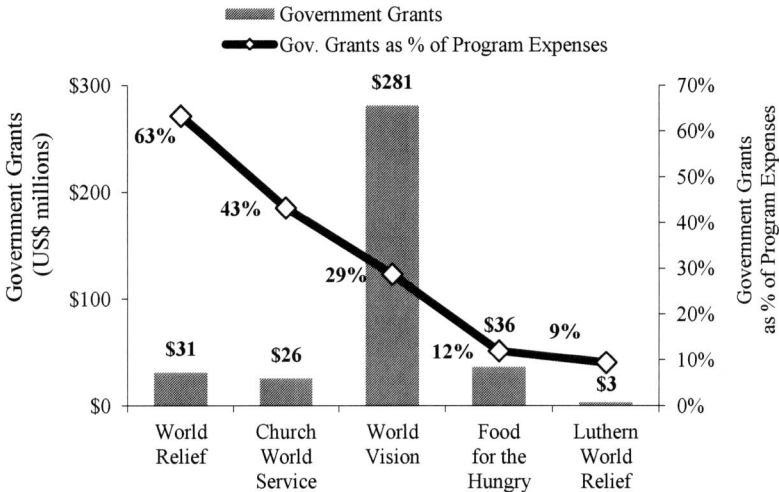

Source: Financial reports of the listed organizations. All data is for 2008
except for Food for the Hungry and Catholic Relief Services where 2007 data
is shown.

Figure 1 Government Funds Received by Select Christian
Organizations

Second wave missionaries also generally hold to a dispensational,

premillennial eschatology while their first wave predecessors

held to a post-millennial eschatology. Belief in premillennial

eschatology has notable political implications because it predicts

political and military events in the Middle East. It is also

connected to Christian Zionist theology which calls Christians to

support the State of Israel politically and militarily. Given its

importance and political ramifications, Christian Zionism will be

examined next.

Eschatology and Christian Zionism

Contemporary mission in the Middle East is occurring against the backdrop of Christian Zionism—a movement that blends religious and political beliefs while offering strong support to the State of Israel, as well as unrelenting support to the expansion of settlements there. Many American churches support both the missions and Zionists movements. In order to better understand the political dynamics surrounding Christian mission work, it is therefore necessary to briefly review evangelical eschatological beliefs and Christian Zionism in particular.

American evangelicals constitute the heart of the contemporary missions movement and generally espouse dispensational premillennialism. This doctrine predicts several events will occur immediately prior to the return of Jesus Christ and the establishment of his thousand-year kingdom. Specifically, it anticipates a coming time-period known as the tribulation during which the world will experience a never-before-seen wave of wars and disasters:

> According to the Bible, there is coming a calamity unlike any which this weary world has even seen. And although this future period will be relatively short, it will nevertheless destroy more of this Earth's population than all previous disasters combined. The estimated toll of human lives lost ranges from 750 million to one billion. An additional 340 million would be seriously injured, and 33 percent of those incapacitated because of radiation, chemical, or biological warfare.[24]

Dispensational premillennialists anticipate the rise of an antichrist—an unspeakably evil ruler that will serve as a chief agent of Satan. The antichrist will govern a global political empire that unites the world economically and attempts to compel all humanity to worship Satan.

Dispensational premillennialism anticipates a military sneak-attack on Israel. A collection of nations that are led by the antichrist will establish a peace treaty with Israel. The nations will not honor the agreement, however, but attack it with overwhelming force. Despite their military strength, God will defeat the attacking armies through divine intervention.

Dispensational premillennialism also predicts Christians will be miraculously removed from the earth prior to these events. Christians will be spared the horrors of the tribulation and suddenly "raptured" or taken up into Heaven. They believe they will then return following the tribulation with Jesus and reign during the thousand-year-period. Importantly, most dispensational-premillennialists believe all of the above events will occur in the near future. The chain of prophetic events is thus expected to begin at any moment and some even speculate that the "terminal generation" (i.e., those who will witness the above events) has already been born.[25]

These core elements of dispensational-premillennial eschatology are widely accepted among American evangelicals and some evangelical leaders have warned against refining predictions to a greater degree of specificity. Reservations expressed by Max Lucado, a popular Christian writer and pastor, serve as a good example:

> Don't be troubled by the return of Christ. Don't be anxious about things you cannot comprehend. Issues like the millennium and the Antichrist are intended to challenge and stretch us, but not overwhelm and divide us. For the Christian, the return of Christ is not a riddle to be solved or a code to be broken, but rather a day to be anticipated.[26]

At the same time, a small group of evangelical leaders, including most Christian Zionists, offer more refined interpretations. These leaders name Russia and Iran as the nations that will attack Israel. The European Union is predicted to be the political base the antichrist will use to build his empire. China is sometimes identified as a key player in the end-times battles.[27]

There are also a small number of evangelical leaders making even more specific predictions. Christian Televangelist Jerry Falwell declared that the antichrist would be Jewish.[28] Joel Richardson, a Christian author of multiple books on Islam, argues that the antichrist will be the Madhi—the anticipated 12th Imam in Shia Islam.[29] Christian novelist Joel Rosenberg predicts Israel will discover vast oil and gas deposits and that Muslims will convert to Christianity *en mass*.[30]

Premillennial eschatological views have widely permeated into American culture.[31] Evidence is seen in the popularity of books like *The Late Great Planet Earth* and the non-fiction, *Left Behind* series which follows a premillennial view of the future. Work by political scientist James Guth and others show the political consequences of the aforementioned perceptions. American evangelicals are more likely to support Israel and a belligerent foreign policy in the Middle East. "Evangelicals, and especially theological dispensationalists, increasingly supported a strong alliance with Israel—one of the few amply demonstrated effects of religious affiliation and doctrine on foreign policy attitudes."[32] Moreover, "All this evidence points to evangelicals as a key source of public support for militant internationalism."[33]

Premillennial eschatology serves as a backdrop to Christian Zionism. John Hagee, one of the most vocal advocates for Christian Zionism, serves as an example. He foresees imminent conflict in the Middle East and believes, "The final battle for Jerusalem is about to begin."[34] He suggests attempts to forge peace agreements are foolhardy. "Israel, desperate for peace, is negotiating itself into the greatest war Israel has even seen. That war will affect every nation on earth, including America, and will affect every person on Planet Earth."[35] Hagee thus calls for a hard line political stance on the part of Israel and America:

> Israel should not give another inch of land to the Palestinians until every terrorist organization operating under the Palestinian cover lay down their weapons of war and prove they are willing to live in peace side by side with the State of Israel. The Palestinians should revise their charter calling for the destruction of Israel. Jerusalem is not to be divided, again, for any reason with

anyone regardless of the requirements of the Roadmap for Peace.[36]

Mike Evans, a best-selling Christian Zionist author provides another illustrative example.[37] His views contain copious references to premillennial eschatology. Israel "seems to stand ready today to take on the world if need be—and she soon may have to." The European Union "can easily be seen as part of the end-time government that will ratify a false seven-year peace agreement with Israel." Russia is "the probable coalition leader of Gog and Magog in biblical prophecy that will sweep down from the North to attack Israel."[38]

While premillennial eschatology provides an important back-drop to the Christian Zionist movement, it does not lie at the heart of the arguments made for supporting Israel. The theological core of the movement is a single verse that records a promise spoken by God to Abraham, the patriarch of the Jewish nation. "I will bless those who bless you, and whoever curses you I will curse."[39] Christian Zionist arguments emphasize and expand on this verse more than they utilize any passages or doctrines central to dispensational premillennialism. For example in his book, *Jerusalem Countdown,* John Hagee offers five Biblical reasons why Christians should support Israel:

1. Israel is the only nation created by a sovereign act of God.

2. Christians owe a debt of eternal gratitude to the Jewish people for their contributions, which gave birth to the Christian faith.

3. Jesus never denied his Jewishness.

4. Christians are to support Israel because it brings the blessings of God to them personally.

5. God judges the Gentiles for their abuse of the Jews.[40]

None of these points directly links with premillennial doctrines. The first three are connected to core Christian beliefs about Jews being the people through whom God offers salvation. The latter two points (to which Hagee notably devotes the most pages) are off-shoots of prosperity theology rather than premillennialism. Prosperity theology holds that God materially blesses those who obey his commands but punishes those who disobey. Hagee's last two points are simply extensions of that idea. Christians will materially be blessed if they politically support Israel but punished if they do not. "Prosperity, divine healing, and the outpouring of the Holy Spirit came first to Gentiles who blessed the Jewish people and the nation of Israel in a practical manner."[41] Conversely, "There will be grave consequences for the nation or nations that attempt to divide up the Land of Israel."[42]

> God promises to punish the nations that come against Israel. America, the Arabs, the European Union, the United Nations, Russia, China—indeed all nations—are in the valley of decision. Every nation that presumes to interfere with God's plan for Israel, including the United States, stands not only against Israel but also ultimately against God. God is rising to judge the nations of the world based on their treatment of the State of Israel.[43]

Mike Evans provides another illustrative example. He draws a strong connection between the material prosperity of the United States and its willingness to support Israel politically. Moreover, he suggests the most challenging struggles of the nation might have been averted with a stronger commitment to Israel:

> Is it possible that American might have been spared the Great Depression if it had not ignored the plight of the Jews? Is it possible that tens of thousands of Americans would not have died in World War II if America had not closed its doors to the house of Israel...
>
> Would September 11 have happened had America maintained moral clarity? I do not believe it would have.
>
> The Great Depression was God's judgment for the bigotry of anti-Semitism...[44]

One reason why Hagee and others ultimately fall back on doctrines that are not directly related to premillennial eschatology is that the latter presents an obvious conundrum as a basis for action. If Biblical prophecies declare these events will happen, is there any point in trying to avert them? Joel Rosenberg touches on this dilemma when discussing his predictions about a coming attack on Israel by Iran and U.S. foreign policy. He ultimately falls back on political rather than prophetic reasoning:

> Q: Do the prophecies... mean that the U.S. should simply accept the inevitable and give up attempts to stop Iran from acquiring nuclear weapons?
>
> A: The answer to this question is no. Even though the Bible makes it clear that Iran will join forces with Russia

and attack Israel, that doesn't mean the U.S. should sit idly by and wait for it to happen. Stopping Tehran from building or acquiring nuclear weapons is essential for the stability and security of the Middle East and the entire world.[45]

Mike Evans also discusses this paradox and argues that America can essentially choose to *become* part of Israel during the end-times cataclysms:

Many believe that there is nothing we can do about it. If it is foretold, then it must come to pass. However, if that is our attitude then we are missing the true point of prophecy. The Bible doesn't tell us what the future holds so that we can sit back and let disaster strike; but rather so that we can prepare, and take any necessary actions to make sure we are on the prophetic side of blessing, and not cursing.

Our position in the last days will be determined by our choice of allegiance: Will the growing liberal tendencies of our nation pull us to join the EU, UN, and Russia in a globalization move that will, in the end, force a false peace on Israel and begin the Tribulation? Or will we, with our moral clarity, large Jewish populace, and Christian consciousness, align ourselves so closely in the final conflict that the U.S. and Israel are literally indistinguishable in the final chapter of biblical prophecy?[46]

To conclude, evangelical perceptions of Israel and the Middle East are influenced by premillennial theology which predicts (among other things) a peace treaty between Israel and the antichrist which is ultimately broken with a military sneak attack. Guth has demonstrated evangelical support for Israel and the Wars in Iraq and Afghanistan are linked to these theological views.[47] Christian Zionism borrows from dispensational premillennial doctrines, but using them as a basis for political action is problematic because of its prophetic nature; the prophecies cannot be averted without invalidating the interpretation. Many key Christian Zionist leaders thus ultimately fall back on prosperity theology to argue that God will materially bless the United States if it politically supports Israel.

Christian Zionism has been encouraged, to an extent, by conservative politicians in Israel. Jerry Falwell, a well recognized Baptist preacher, staunch supporter of Israel, and co-founder of the Moral Majority, offers one of the earliest examples. Prime Minister Menachem Begin (of the Likud Party) invited Falwell to Israel in 1978 and invited him back again the next year. In 1980, Begin gave Falwell the Jabotinsky Centennial Medal for friendship to Israel and a private jet. Many other Prime Ministers would latter meet with Falwell including Yitzhak Shamir, Yitzhak Rabin, Shimon Peres, Benjamin Netanyahu, and Ariel Sharon. Falwell was not alone and the Ministry of Tourism reached out to many evangelical leaders and provided them with a free trip to Israel.[48] Another Likud Prime Minister, Benjamin Netanyahu, brought 17 Christian leaders to Israel in 1996. The group issued a statement supporting Israeli settlements in the Occupied Territories and launched an ad campaign for a united Jerusalem under Israeli control.[49] In 2002 Ehud Olmert, a future Prime Minister who was then serving as the Mayor of Jerusalem, co-chaired the "Praying for Jerusalem" campaign with American televangelist Pat Robertson.[50] John Hagee frequently meets and speaks with Israeli political leaders. At a 2010 Christians United for Israel (CUFI) Summit in Israel, Benjamin Netanyahu heaped praise on him:

> Christian Zionism preceded modern Jewish Zionism, and I think enabled it. But it received a tremendous impetus several decades ago when leading American clergymen, among them most notably, Pastor John Hagee, a dynamic pastor and leader from Texas, began to say to their congregations and to anyone who listened, it's time to take a stand with Israel.[51]

Mike Evans has similarly been encouraged. Benjamin Netanyahu said, "The tens of millions of Christians who fervently support Israel are fortunate to have your passionate and dedicated voice helping them understand the critical issues that face the one and only Jewish State." Ehud Olmert called Evans a "true ambassador of Jerusalem representing millions of Christians in America."[52]

Encouraging Christian Zionism yields obvious political dividends for the State of Israel. Menachem Begin called on Jerry Falwell to "get to work for me" after Israeli bombed Iraq's nuclear reactor in 1981.[53] Prime Minister Ariel Sharon told a gathering of Christian Zionists, "We need you and we need your support."[54] Beyond the political benefits, the Christian Zionist movement has brought economic benefits. John Hagee Ministries has donated over $60 million towards humanitarian causes in Israel.[55]

Christian tourism brings additional economic benefits. The Ministry of Tourism reported over one million "Christian pilgrims" went to Israel in 2008—a number representing one third of all tourists to Israel. Thirty percent of the Christian pilgrims, moreover, came from the United States. Not all of these visitors, of course, are Christian Zionists but Christian Zionist groups actively promote tourism which is a $3 billion dollar industry for Israel.[56] A wide range of tour operators, hoteliers, and others thus economically benefit from the Christian Zionist movement.

While eschatological views are certainly in the backdrop of American mission work in Israel/Palestine, they do not strongly influence expectations, methods, and self-perceptions of the missionaries themselves. Efforts and methods there are similar to those made elsewhere. Among the missionaries interviewed, none claimed that evangelizing Israel/Palestine was more important than evangelizing other areas of the globe; several had worked outside the Middle East or mentioned an openness to do so. Practical considerations temper expectations. For example, one interviewee stated that mass conversion was "out of the question."[57] Another emphasized that working in Israel demands great patience because conversions are few and far between.[58] Stated goals are limited. Simply removing obstacles to evangelism ("rocks" in the missionary parlance) is in itself considered a victory. Building friendships and trust between Christians and non-Christians are understood as crucial first steps in sharing the Gospel. Likewise, opportunities to present the Gospel (typically in one-on-one fashion) are considered victories regardless of how the message is received. The occasional convert represents a rare reward for their efforts. Only one interviewee expressed a more ambitious goal of establishing a community of Christian believers in every village in the Middle East and even this individual acknowledged the difficulties of achieving such an end.[59]

The limited influence premillennial eschatology has on second wave mission expectations contrasts sharply with the strong influence post-millennial eschatology had on first wave expectations. As discussed in Chapter One, first wave missionaries felt a sense of urgency and invincibility due to post-millennial predictions of an imminent era of global, Christian dominance. They believed their efforts would ultimately succeed and hasten the coming of the millennium. Their defeats were merely setbacks preceding a wider, inevitable victory. Most second wave missionaries, on the other hand, have no preconceived expectations for success because they anticipate an imminent era of global, Christian persecution.[60] Their successes merely precede a wider, inevitable defeat which will be followed by an ultimate victory won by Christ, supernaturally. Having broadly outlined second wave mission work and its underlining theology I will now present three case studies beginning with one on Iraqi Kurds. Each case study will identify areas in which politics influenced mission work and vice versa.

[1] See Handy, "American Religious Depression" for an excellent discussion of this period of American church history and its consequences on the missions movement.

[2] Anderson, "American Protestants," 105.

[3] Figures include Canadian missionaries; Ibid., 108; Linda J. Webber, etc. Mission Handbook: U.S. and Canadian Protestant Ministries Overseas (Wheaton, Billy Graham Center, 2010), 38.

[4] PCUSA General Assembly Mission Council, e-mail message to author, Dallas, August 20, 2011; See also: http://gamc.pcusa.org/ministries/world-mission/

[5] Ibid.

[6] The American Baptist Missionary Union was the mission board of the Northern Baptists.

[7] William H. Brackney, *Baptist in North America: A Historical Perspective*, (Malden: Blackwell Publishing, 2006), 214; Webber, Mission Handbook, 99.

[8] Ibid., 291.

[9] Ibid., 115; Between 1906 and 1915 William J. Seymour, an African-American preacher, led a series of revival meetings on Azusa Street in Los Angeles. The Pentecostal, Assemblies of God denomination grew out of the revivals in 1914 and mission efforts began shortly thereafter.

[10] Ibid., 129.

[11] Campus Crusade for Christ, "A Place of Destiny" http://joinus.campuscrusadeforchrist.com/ why-campus-ministry/a-place-of-destiny/ (accessed May 5, 2012).

[12] Weber, *Mission Handbook*, 258.

[13] Ibid., 267; Although it is a major American mission organization, Partners International does not field American missionaries but rather supports indigenous leaders.

[14] World Vision, "Who We Are" http://www.worldvision.org/resources.nsf/Main/annual-review-2011-resources/$FILE/ar2011-financial-highlights.pdf (accessed May 5, 2012).

[15] Mission historian William Hutchison estimates that these boards accounted for 80% of all mission activity; Hutchison, Errand to the World, 45.

[16] J. Bruce Nichols, *The Uneasy Alliance: Religion, Refugee Work, and U.S. Foreign Policy*, (New York: Oxford University Press, 1988), 24.

[17] Ibid., 25.

[18] Ibid., 25-26; A substantial portion of the ABCFM's resources and efforts were directed towards American Indians. For example in its 1836 annual report, 18% of the ABCFM's budget was devoted to work among the

American Indians. Work in the Middle East, by comparison, accounted for 27%; ABCFM, *1836 Annual Report,* (Boston: ABCFM, 1986), 120-123.

[19] Nichols, *The Uneasy Alliance,* 38; Notably, Herbert Hoover was a Quaker.

[20] Ibid., 55, 68.

[21] The United States Agency of International Development (USAID) describes the policy as follows: "Grant funds may not be used for inherently religious activities such as worship, prayer, proselytizing, or devotional Bible study. The funds are to be used to further the objectives established by Congress such as economic development, food aid, fighting disease, disaster relief, as well as other USAID stated programs and goals. Recipients of the development program and assistance may not be selected by reference to religion. The religious affiliation of the recipient cannot be taken into account in advertising or delivering services. Faith-based organizations are required to serve people of all faiths or people of no faith in any program that they administer with Federal dollars. Faith-based organizations may not use Federal funds to purchase religious materials - such as the Bible, Torah, Koran, or other religious or scriptural materials."; USAID, "Faith-Based Organizations FAQ" http://www.usaid.gov/work-usaid/faith-based-organizations/faith-based-organizations-faq#Q7 (accessed June 8, 2012).

[22] The fundamentals of Christianity are formulated in various ways but generally include the following: The Bible is the inspired, inerrant word of God; There is one, triune God; Jesus Christ was born of a virgin, crucified, bodily resurrected, and was both fully human and God; All people fell from grace as a result of their own actions and are in need to salvation; The saved will spend eternity in Heaven while the lost will spend eternity in Hell; Jesus Christ's crucifixion and resurrection provides the only path to spiritual salvation. For examples see the statement of beliefs from the leading mission organizations; Southern Baptist Convention, "Basic Beliefs," http://www.sbc.org/aboutus/basicbeliefs.asp (accessed June 8, 2012); Assemblies of God USA, "Assemblies of God Fundamental Truths," http://ag.org/top/Beliefs/ Statement_of_Fundamental_Truths/sft_short.cfm (accessed June 8, 2012); World Vision, "Christian Commitment," http://www.worldvision.org/content.nsf/about/hr-faith (accessed June 8, 2012); New Tribes Mission, "What We Believe," http://usa.ntm.org/what-we-believe (accessed June 8, 2012); Campus Crusade for Christ, "Statement of Faith," http://www.ccci.org/about-us/statement-of-faith/index.htm (accessed June 8, 2012).

[23] Fundamentalists/evangelical organizations began to dominate the mission field in the late 1950s. In 1952, 50% of North American Protestant missionaries were connected to mainline mission boards. By 1958, the figure had declined to 41%. Organizations unaffiliated with mainline churches,

conversely, grew 9% over the same time period; Anderson, "American Protestants," 108.

[24] Mark Bailey, "The Tribulation," in *The Road to Armageddon,* Charles Swindoll et. al. (Nashville: Thomas Nelson Publishers, 2004), 50.

[25] John Hagee is an excellent example. He argued this generation would see the return of Christ in his book, *Beginning Of The End;* John Hagee. Beginning Of The End: The Assassination of Yitzhak Rabin and the Coming Antichrist, (Nashville: Thomas Nelson Inc., 1996).

[26] Max Lucado, *When Christ Comes* (Nashville: Thomas Nelson Publishers, 2001), 5.

[27] For examples of this see: John Walvoord, *Armageddon, Oil and Terror* (Carol Stream: Tyndale House Publishers, 2007); David Jerimiah, What in the World is Going On? 10 Prophetic Clues You Cannot Afford to Ignore (Nashville: Thomas Nelson, 2008); Hal Lindsey, *The Late Great Planet Earth* (Grand Rapids: Zondervan, 1970).

[28] Debra Nussbaum Cohen, "Falwell Antichrist remark sparks anti-Semitism charges," Jweekly.com, http://www.jweekly.com/includes/print/9993/article/falwell-antichrist-remark-sparks-anti-semitism-charges/ (accessed November 26, 2011).

[29] Joel Richardson, *The Islamic Antichrist: The Shocking Truth about the Real Nature of the Beast*, (Washington: WND Books, 2009).

[30] Joel C. Rosenberg, *Epicenter: Why The Current Rumblings in the Middle East Will Change your Future* (Carol Stream: Tyndale House Publishers, 2006).

[31] For more on this see Paul Boyer, *When Time Shall Be No More* (Boston: Belknap Press of Harvard University Press, 1994).

[32] James Guth, "Religion and American Attitudes on Foreign Policy," (paper, International Studies Association, New York, NY, February 15-17, 2009), 10.

[33] Ibid., 16.

[34] John Hagee, *Jerusalem Countdown: A Warning to the World* (Lake Mary: Frontline, 2006), 3.

[35] Ibid., 24-25.

[36] Ibid., 26.

[37] Notably, Mike Evans was born to a non-practicing Jewish mother and became a Christian as a child. Evans also claims to have anointed Benjamin Netanyahu with oil and predicted he would twice become the Prime Minister of Israel.

[38] Mike Evans, *The American Prophecies: Ancient Scriptures Reveal Our Nation's Future* (New York: Warner Faith, 2004), 160-162.

[39] Genesis 12:3 (NIV Translation)

[40] Hagee, *Jerusalem Countdown*, 196-201.

[41] Ibid., 198.

[42] Ibid., 194.

[43] Ibid., 201.

[44] Evans, *The American Prophecies*, 212, 214, 244.

[45] Rosenberg, *Epicenter*, p. 245.

[46] Evans, *The American Prophecies*, 15, 163.

[47] James Guth, "Religion and American Attitudes on Foreign Policy."

[48] Timothy P. Weber, On the Road to Armageddon: How Evangelicals Became Israel's Best Friend (Grand Rapids: Baker Academic, 2004), 214; Don Wagner, "For Zion's Sake," *Middle East Report* 233 (Summer, 2002), 52-57.

[49] Donald Wagner, "The Evangelical-Jewish Alliance," *Claremont School of Theology: Religion Online.org* http://www.religion-online.org/showarticle.asp?title=2717 (accessed November 26, 2011).

[50] "Pat Robertson forms alliance with mayor of Jerusalem," *The Baptist Standard*, November 11, 2002 http://www.baptiststandard.com/2002/11_11/print/robertson.html (accessed November 26, 2011).

[51] CUFI was founded by Pastor John Hagee and is one of the most prominent, Christian Zionist organizations.

Benjamin Netanyahu, "PM Netanyahu's Address to the Christians United For Israel Jerusalem Summit," *netanyayu.org.il*, August 8, 2010 http://en.netanyahu.org.il/news/300/243/PM-Netanyahu-%E2%84%A2s-Address-to-the-Christians-United-For-Israel-Jerusalem-Summit/ (accessed November 27, 2011).

[52] "About Dr. Mike Evans," Jerusalem Prayer Team, http://jerusalemprayerteam.org/ AboutDrMikeEvans.asp (accessed November 26, 2011).

[53] In 1981, Israel launched a surprise air-strike against an Iraqi nuclear reactor. The reactor had been purchased from France and Iraq maintained it would be used for peaceful purposes. The airstrike heavily damaged the reactor but caused considerable international controversy.

[54] John J. Mearscheimer and Stephen M. Walt, *The Israeli Lobby and U.S. Foreign Policy* (New York: Farrar, Straus and Giroux), 2007.

[55] "Pastor John C. Hagee," John Hagee Ministries, http://www.jhm.org/Home/ About/PastorJohnHagee (accessed November 26, 2011).

[56] Israel Ministry of Tourism, *A Pilgrimage to the Holy Land – A Bridge for Peace: Christian Tourism to Israel*, April 2009; The Central Bureau of Statistics, *Tourism in Israel 1990-2009,* January 2011.

[57] Interview with individual involved in mission work in the Middle East, Ft. Worth, TX, October 21, 2011.

[58] Telephone interview with individual involved in mission work in the Middle East, Dallas, TX, October 15, 2011.

[59] Interview with individual involved in mission work in the Middle East, Dallas, TX, November 1, 2011.

[60] Missionaries to Iran are a notable exception. See chapter six for more on this.

Chapter 3: Case Study on Iraqi Kurds

During the first wave of mission work in the 1800s and early 1900s, American organizations established a notable presence in Northern Iraq which was then part of the Ottoman Empire. By 1859, there were roughly a dozen American missionaries spread across Urmia, Seir, Gawar, and Mosul.[1] By 1900, there were over one hundred schools instructing over 2,400 students.[2] Little effort was made to reach the Kurds, however. The "Great Experiment" strategy targeted Christians rather than Muslims, and Kurds were not evangelized with one exception. Roger Cumberland worked among them beginning in 1923 until he was killed by Kurds in 1938.

By the mid 1900s, the first wave of American missionary effort to the region tapered off. The 1958 coup in Iraq brought most of the lingering work to an end; the new anti-Western government quickly expelled the remaining missionaries. By 1959, only four remained in Northern Iraq. The Ba'athist coup in 1968 erased even these last vestiges of a once a substantial presence.[3] Between 1968 and the 1991, there were no American missionaries in Northern Iraq.

Circumstances dramatically changed following the Gulf War and George H. W. Bush's calls for the overthrow of Saddam Hussein. The Kurds rebelled against a weakened and disoriented Iraqi army and although they gained some initial ground, the army quickly regrouped and crushed the uprising through the use of helicopter gunships. This provoked fears of reprisals and one million Kurdish refugees fled north to the cold, barren, Turkish border. A humanitarian disaster ensued with an estimated 800-1,000 Kurds dying daily.[4]

The U.S. responded with operation Provide Comfort and the creation of a "no-fly" zone in Northern Iraq. The U.N. likewise, for the first time in history, stripped a nation of sovereign control over part of its territory. American ground forces provided security temporarily; American aircraft kept the Iraqi military at bay. International NGOs arrived to assist the refugees and with them came the first opportunity in nearly fifty years for outside Christian groups to operate in Northern Iraq. Grants from the U.S. government and other entities notably complemented relief funds raised from private sources.

By 1996, there were an estimated 60 permanent American missionaries in Northern Iraq.[5] Most of these worked for NGOs that were providing humanitarian assistance. They were also supplemented by a small number of short-term workers including (on one occasion) Tom Coburn, a doctor from Muskogee Oklahoma who became a member of the U.S. Congress in 1994 and a member of the U.S. Senate in 2004.[6]

Escalated fighting between the two main Kurdish political parties, the PUK and the KDP, closed the window of opportunity for American missionaries five years later. The U.S. had brokered a peace agreement between the two after the Gulf War but initial skirmishes in the summer of 1996 led to full-scale fighting. In August, the KDP invited Saddam's forces into the North to help it root the PUK out of Irbil. In the process, it also betrayed the CIA-backed operations in the city, shattering any immediate hopes of ousting Saddam.[7]

This "deal with the devil" prompted the U.S. to hastily closes its small command post in Northern Iraq and conclude operation Provide Comfort. A description of the abandoned post illustrates the frantic nature of the withdrawal:

> What the Americans left behind when they pulled out the Military Coordinating Center in the frontier town of Zakho is instructive—and sad. The detritus of international altruism gone awry included 32 personal weapons, computers, a radio still turned on, three HumVee all-terrain vehicles, a larger number of ordinary cars, maps, diverse sensitive documents and a small library of spy thriller novels.[8]

The loss of American protection was just the first challenge of continuing mission work in Northern Iraq. Infighting between the KDP and PUK destabilized security conditions as did interventions by Turkey and Iran.[9] It also became increasingly difficult for aid workers to use the Turkish-Iraqi border and the U.S. State Department began pressuring American NGOs to withdraw.[10] The 1996 U.S. Presidential election was only months away and the Clinton administration feared a hostage crisis would have adverse political consequences. In the end, all of the Americans left.

The Kurds that had worked with the American NGOs feared Saddam's incursion would lead to reprisals. They began lobbying for assistance and, in the fall of 1996, the U.S. launched operation Pacific Haven which evacuated approximately 6,600 Kurds out of Iraq.[11] The evacuated Kurds were resettled in the United States and included among them were Kurds that had worked closely with the American missionaries during the inter-war period. The second phase of contemporary American missionary effort was thus brought to a close.

The beginning of the Iraq War in 2003 once again dramatically changed circumstances. Kurdish ground forces, in cooperation with the U.S. military, pushed Saddam's troops out of the north.[12] The quick collapse of the Iraqi government and subsequent U.S. occupation gave the north a larger measure of autonomy and security. Most of the resistance to the occupation was likewise outside of the north creating a haven of relative tranquility.

The Kurdish Regional Government had an open-door policy for foreign NGOs seeking to operate within the region. Organizations with overt missionary aims were not welcomed, but any group, regardless of their religious convictions, could come and undertake humanitarian projects. Foreigners were also allowed to work in the region. This created an opportunity for

American missionaries to return and an estimated 80 workers were present in Northern Iraq by 2010.[13]

Many contemporary mission organizations are focusing their efforts on educational ventures, a pattern similar to the first-wave missionaries that came to the region a century earlier. Servant Group International, for example, has founded three private Christian schools which boast 1,500 students.[14] Another organization, Global Hope, is likewise building a "Freedom Center Iraq" facility which will host English and professional development classes.[15] A Florida-based Baptist church is part of an international group establishing a Baptist Cultural Center in Dohuk, Iraq. Brian Barlow, the missions pastor at the church said the new center would teach "the universal principles of kindness, respect, compassion, human rights, charity, dignity, equality, and peaceful co-existence."[16] Interviewees also reported that mission-minded Americans are coming to Northern Iraq and serving as teachers in public and private schools.

Efforts by American mission organizations are having little impact on the religious landscape. Most of the missionaries interviewed reported that Muslim Kurds are open to discussing religion and Christianity but few are willing to change faiths. Conversions are rare and only one missionary reported a case of quick congregational growth where the number of converts doubled from 100 to 200 within a few years. The total religious impact of the past two decades of missionary efforts is difficult to gauge with much certainty. Social pressures combined with the ever-present threats of physical violence discourage Kurdish converts from openly expressing their religious convictions. There is one officially recognized church for Kurdish converts, the Kurdzman Church of Christ. (The congregation's building was notably financed in part by World Compassion, a Tulsa-based Christian ministry.) In addition, there are an estimated 20 unofficial groups that meet within private homes.[17] Estimates of the total number of Kurdish converts generally range from 300-1,000.[18]

Some interviewees reported that the growth of nascent Christian groups is inhibited by internal disputes among Kurdish converts. One in particular said that missionaries are partly to blame. Kurdish church-leaders derive prestige and resources through their association with foreign missionaries. A form of resource-politics can occur as a result, with Kurds competing for and controlling relationships. The variety of foreign groups present in the country can also foster factional splits by (knowingly or unknowingly) supporting break-away members of established congregations.

Impact of Mission Work on International Politics

The missionaries who came to Northern Iraq after the Gulf War have had little influence on American foreign policy relative to their first wave peers. In large part, this is because other concerns such as oil, nuclear proliferation, terrorism and the Mid-East peace process have dominated the U.S. agenda. These concerns were non-existent during the early years of the 20th century leaving the missionaries as the chief American concern. Most of the contemporary missionaries have kept a low political profile but some have publically voiced political opinions. One example is James Jennings. In 1991 after the Gulf War, he founded Conscience International which helped operate a medical clinic for the Kurdish refugees in Northern Iraq. The organization went on to bring medical teams and supplies to Iraq both before and after the Iraq War.[19] During the inter-war period, Jennings became an outspoken opponent of the economic sanctions and the Iraq War. In 2000, Conscience International joined with the Mennonite Central Committee, the Presbyterian Church USA, and the United Methodist Church to form Compassion Iraq—a collation of Christian groups opposed to the economic sanctions. Serving as the coalition's director Jennings said, "Christians should be pushing to end the embargo... Jesus taught that we should love our enemies, not starve them into submission."[20] In 2001, Conscience International defied the U.S. no-fly zone and organized a "Baghdad Airlift" which brought a group of 70 Americans to Baghdad along with medicines, books, and school supplies.[21] In 2002, Conscience organized a group of American activists who journeyed from the Jordanian border across the desert into Iraq. The "Peace Walk" opposed the looming Iraq War and the economic sanctions. "It is time to end this failed policy, not to start a new war."[22] The group's pleas went unheeded and the U.S. followed-through with its invasion plans.

Servant Group International (SGI) is another organization that has publically engaged in advocacy efforts. The Tennessee-based SGI was founded in 1992 to assist thousands of Kurdish refugees that were resettled to Nashville following Saddam's Anfal campaign. [23] SGI was one of the many organizations that began relief and development operations in Northern Iraq after the Gulf War. In 1995, the group's founder, Doug Layton, testified before the U.S. congress on the plight of Iraqi Kurds and urged the U.S. government to protect them:

> When Hitler was asked how he thought he might get away with the final solution, he replied that the world had done nothing about the Armenians, and they would do nothing about the Jews. The question is what will we do today about the Kurds? As a committed Christian, I have asked myself what must God think about all of this, and the scripture that comes to my mind is in Proverbs, Chapter 24, verse 11. It says, "Rescue those being led away to death, hold back those staggering towards slaughter. If you say, but we knew nothing about this, does He who weighs the heart not perceive it? Does he who guards your life not know it? Will not He repay a person according to what he has done?"[24]

Following the Iraq War, Layton lobbied for business investment into the region. He served as the Country Director for the Kurdistan Development Corporation which was a private/public partnership backed by the Kurdish Regional Government. He and former SGI chairman William Galloway produced a series of advertisements that were aired in the U.S.

and U.K. in an effort to attract investment and tourism. The ads showed Kurds thanking Americans and Britons for ousting Saddam and depicted the region as peaceful and economically vibrant.[25] Their efforts had limited success and Layton left the group after two years to head The Other Iraq Tours—a company that works closely with the KRG Directorate of Tourism to encourage travel to Kurdistan.[26]

Discreet advocacy efforts have complemented public efforts and yielded more results. Following the end of Operation Provide Comfort and the withdrawal of U.S. protection from Northern Iraq, some of the missionaries quietly advocated on behalf of the Kurds that were seeking to flee the country. Their efforts, in part, led to Operation Pacific Haven—the American military operation that evacuated 6,000 Kurds from Northern Iraq and resettled them into the U.S. Of note is that many Kurds were resettled to Nashville, home of SGI.

The most important foreign policy issue facing the Kurds is the question of an independent Kurdish state. The circumstances are very similar to those that surrounded the question of Armenian independence in the 1920s. Both groups were lacking a state of their own. Both groups were persecuted by the authorities that governed them. In both cases, moreover, wars fought for unrelated reasons raised the possibility of nationhood. It could be expected, therefore, that contemporary American missionaries, like their predecessors from earlier years, would strongly favor independence. This is not the case. Most of the missionaries interviewed were sympathetic to the Kurdish cause but also acutely aware of the geo-political implications of nationhood. Many expressed concerns that independence would only worsen the Kurds' situation by inviting war with Turkey and Iran. Only a few unequivocally asserted that the Kurds should have an independent state of their own.

Impact of International Politics on Mission Work

U.S. policy towards Iraq has clearly had a tremendous impact on the missionary efforts to Iraqi Kurds. First and foremost, it opened, shut, and re-opened the door to missionary activities. The creation of the "safe haven" following the Gulf War allowed missionaries to enter the region after a 30 year hiatus. The withdrawal of the U.S., in turn, re-closed the door that would be opened once again following the Iraq War. Had it not been for the U.S. intervention into the region, American missionaries would not have been able to establish a presence in Iraq.

U.S. policy has also benefited the missionaries in other ways. During the Inter-war period, government grants helped fund the humanitarian projects undertaken by Christian (and other) NGOs. The degree of dependence on such funds varied. One missionary reported that his organization was only able to establish a long-term presence in Northern Iraq because of the availability of government funding. Another reported that his organization was essentially funded by American donors but was able to obtain new equipment through a government grant. In any event, government money bolstered the operations of many Christian and secular NGO groups. It also provided funds for security guards to help protect the NGO workers carrying out grant-projects.

Missionaries received less formal forms of assistance from the U.S. government as well, particularly at the start of the inter-war period when U.S. ground forces had a notable presence in Northern Iraq. Christian workers were able to obtain transport on U.S. military vehicles at times and the military brought in food, water, and other supplies which were shared with NGO workers. When harassed by hostile Iraqi forces the missionaries (like other expatriate workers) could seek help from the U.S. military. In one of the more colorful examples of this, a missionary team was being attacked by mortar-fire from a near-by Republican Guard unit. The U.S. military commander, upon hearing of the situation, ordered an F-15 fighter to buzz the Iraqi forces at low altitude. Catching the hint, the Republican Guard units quickly ceased firing and withdrew.

The evacuation of Kurds that followed the end of Operation Provide Comfort provides another example of the intertwining of politics and missionary efforts. Operation Pacific Haven allowed the missionaries to help the Kurds that had helped them during the inter-war period by providing asylum visas and resettlement into the United States. Such a move bolstered the reputation of the missionary teams and offered a substantial

benefit to association with them. One (non-missionary) observer
suggested that the Kurds exploited the situation in Northern Iraq
following Operation Provide Comfort and manipulated the
Americans that had been operating there:

> All Kurds, without exception, want asylum in the United
> States… Certain individuals were able to manipulate
> situation reports to create an environment where getting
> asylum was a certainty. It is not going too far to say that
> the Americans were duped. In this case, it also created a
> climate of fear in a vacuum—and it will be very difficult
> for them to come back.[27]

The close cooperation between the U.S. government and
NGOs (secular and Christian alike) came to an end during the
inter-war period. Following 2003, the American government's
attention was focused further south. A South Korean detachment
was responsible for peacekeeping in Northern Iraq and there were
few U.S. military personnel there. The government-funded-
NGO-projects likewise gave way to contracts with for-profit
businesses. Christian NGOs had to rely on their own financial
resources and operate more independently from the U.S.
government.

U.S. policy continues to have a lingering impact on
missionary efforts there. Almost all of those interviewed posit
that Kurds have particularly favorable views of Americans
because of U.S. policy towards Iraq and the assistance provided
during the refugee crisis. One interviewee said Kurds will often
state, "The U.S. saved us when we were about to die." The
overthrow of Saddam was celebrated by the Kurds given the past

abuses of his government. Kurds are thus very friendly towards Americans and open to engaging Americans in conversations. Such conversations do not necessarily lead to religious conversions, but the openness stands in stark contrast to attitudes elsewhere. In the words of one interviewee, "Northern Iraq is the only place in the Muslim world where being an American is an asset."

The Iraqi government has also had a notable impact on mission work. The government of Saddam Hussein did not look favorably on foreign missionary efforts. His Ba'athist coup erased the last vestiges of missionary efforts to the country. During the inter-war period, Saddam attempted to curtail the efforts of foreign NGOs in Northern Iraq. He initially acceded to the presence of aid workers but reversed this policy in 1993 declaring any foreign humanitarian work to be illegal. In any event, visas had never been issued to aid workers—they simply crossed the Turkish border. Iraqi military units would occasionally threaten them only to be checked by U.S. airpower. Saddam's government also tried to forestall NGO work by offering bounties. One interviewee reported a six month wave of car bombings in Dohuk that was triggered when Saddam's government offered 10,000 dinars for every bomb. By some accounts, $10,000 - $25,000 was offered for every foreign worked killed. Another interviewee was skeptical that such sums were ever really made available. It may have been offered as an incentive for violence, but the true sums delivered may have been

much less considering the impoverished conditions in Northern
Iraq. In any event, many interviewees reported that lives were
threatened on several occasions and some workers were
physically harmed. None reported any fatalities.

The supreme irony of Saddam's opposition to foreign
missionary efforts is that his own actions provided the biggest, if
unintended, boost to them. His brazen invasion of Kuwait
obviously set the stage for U.S. intervention and his stand-off
with the U.S. a decade latter made the second intervention
politically feasible. Both wars, as discussed above, ultimately
opened the door to American missionary efforts in Iraq. The
genocidal Anfal campaign against the Kurds in 1988-1989
arguably had an even greater impact.

During the Iran-Iraq war in the 1980s, Iran opened up a
northern front against Iraq with the help of Kurdish guerillas.
Saddam ultimately responded in 1988 with the brutal Anfal
campaign against the Kurdish civilian population. All human
beings and animals found in areas outside of government control
were to be killed. Blanket execution orders were given for any
males between the ages of 15 and 70. Over 1,000 Kurdish
villages were destroyed and estimates on the death toll range
from 50,000 – 200,000.[28] The numbers themselves, however, do
not fully illustrate the ferocity of the operations. Kurds were
herded into concentration camps where the men were
systematically separated from the women and children and
executed. Iraqi units raped women and pillaged anything the

Kurds had of value. Young Kurdish women were sold as slaves to men in Iraq, Saudi Arabia and Kuwait.[29] The use of chemical weapons on the village of Halabja punctuated the campaign and left lingering genetic effects on the Kurdish population. Dr. Christine Gosden visited the city ten years after the attack and reported on the impact:

> What I found was far worse than anything I had suspected, devastating problems occurring 10 years after the attack. These chemicals seriously affected people's eyes and respiratory and neurological systems. Many became blind. Skin disorders which involve severe scarring are frequent, and many progress to skin cancer. Working in conjunction with the doctors in the area, I compared the frequency of these conditions such as infertility, congenital malformations and cancers (including skin, head, neck, respiratory system, gastrointestinal tract, breast and childhood cancers) in those who were in Halabja at the time with an unexposed population from a city in the same region. We found the frequencies in Halabja are at least three to four times greater, even 10 years after the attack. An increasing number of children are dying each year of leukemias and lymphomas. The cancers tend to occur in much younger people in Halabja than elsewhere, and many people have aggressive tumors, so that mortality rates are high. No chemotherapy or radiotherapy is available in this region...
>
> On the first day of my visit to the labor and gynecological ward in the hospital, there were no women in normal labor and no one had recently delivered a normal baby. Three women had just miscarried. The staff in the labor ward told of the very large proportion of pregnancies in which there were major malformations. In addition to fetal losses and prenatal deaths, there is also a very large number of infant deaths. The frequencies of these in the Halabjan women are more than four times greater than

that in the neighboring city of Soulemaneya. The findings of serious congenital malformations with genetic causes occurring in children born years after the chemical attack suggest that the effects from these chemical warfare agents are transmitted to succeeding generations.[30]

The campaign left an indelible scar on the Kurdish people and fostered a deeply-rooted hatred of Saddam in particular and Arabs in general. Most of the missionaries interviewed said the campaign has made Kurds more willing to consider Christianity. Saddam and almost all Arab Iraqis profess to be Muslims and the "Anfal" campaign itself derived its name from the eighth sura of the Koran—a passage dealing with the battle of Muslims against non-believers. Many Kurds thus associate the campaign with Islam and persecution by Arabs.

The Anfal campaign also took place against the backdrop of a longer, wider historical legacy of tensions between Kurds and other Muslim ethnic groups, namely the Turks and the Persians. The Kurds remain the largest ethnic group in the world without an independent state and they are spread across Turkey, Iran, Iraq and Syria. In almost every country there have been conflicts between the Kurds and the ruling majorities. During the 1980s and 1990s, the Turkish government launched a massive military effort to root out PKK rebels in Southeast Turkey.

The historical legacy stands in sharp contrast to the humanitarian assistance provided by the West after the Gulf War. One interviewee said Kurds will often tell an illustrative story to highlight the difference. During the refugee crisis, an American soldier apparently witnessed a Turkish soldier abusing a Kurd. In anger, the American punched the Turk to make him stop, humiliating him in front of a large group of Kurds. The story is unverifiable but commonly told all the same as an example of how the Kurds have been mistreated by their Muslim neighbors but helped by outsiders.

The tensions between Kurds and other Muslim groups have fostered deep Kurdish resentment. Frustration with Muslim neighbors, in turn, has led to some disillusionment with Islam. One missionary described the attitude as, "What has Islam done for us?" Interviewees said the Kurds still consider themselves to be Muslim but that the Anfal campaign and wider occurrences of persecution has forged a Kurdish identity based more on ethnicity than religion. Kurds see themselves as Kurds first and foremost rather than Muslims; most interviewees report that, rightly or wrongly, the Kurds believe that they were forced to convert to Islam after being subsumed into the Umayyad Dynasty in the 600s. This distinct identity has not led to wide-spread conversions, but most interviewees report that a greater willingness to consider Christianity, a greater acceptance of converts and a more secular attitude towards Islam is because of the historical legacy of persecution by other Muslims.

The relative measure of religious tolerance is evidenced in many ways. Most of the interviewees said that there is little "official" persecution of Christian converts in Northern Iraq— any government action likely results from the whims of a single individual. Northern Iraq is home to one of the only legally recognized Christian churches for Muslim-background believers. The Kurdish Regional Government has also allowed one Christian organization to sell bibles and give away religiously inspired calendars.

Public comments by KRG officials echo this attitude. At a speech before an inter-faith conference, the former Prime Minister of the KRG, Nechirvan Idris Barzani, cited the common persecution suffered by those of all faiths and the need for religious toleration:

> The chemical weapons which were used against our people did not discriminate among Muslims, Christians, Yezidis, or among Kurds, Assyrians, Chaldeans, Syriacs, or Turkmen. Or between men, women and children. Very brutally, according to a well-formulated plan, the weapons killed everyone...

> The divine religion of Christianity is one of the major religions of the world today and remains continuously in dialogue with Islam. Today Assyrian, Chaldean, Syriac, and Armenian Christians are all citizens of the Kurdistan Region, side by side with us.

> We in the Kurdistan Regional Government support the wishes of our people and we will not allow the valuable religious and social fabric of our people to be weakened or disintegrate...

> Religious tolerance is the symbol of all civilized and successful societies. The Universal Declaration of Human Rights very clearly emphasizes the fact that all nations and countries must support religious freedom and respect the rights of all people to select their religion and worship.

Therefore it is important that all of us in a position of responsibility – whether religious leaders, political or social leaders, or leaders in the fields of media, civil society or the private sector – all emphasize the shared vision for a better and a brighter future. And for all of us to stand firmly against efforts which aim at discrimination and mistrust within our society.[31]

Social attitudes also offer evidence that, while there is still persecution of Christians, it is less severe than is witnessed in many other Muslim societies. The interviewees report that Kurds are largely willing to tolerate Christians that are born into their faith. (As evidence of this, native Christians have been fleeing from the Arab dominated portions of Iraq into Kurdish areas because of persecution.) Interviewees also report a modest measure of tolerance for converts in the sense that most Kurds are willing to overlook conversions unless they occur among those they are close to socially. For example, many employers fire workers that convert to Christianity; landlords will likewise evict tenants that convert and refuse to lease housing to them. Familial relationships are the most sensitive. Families generally bear a social stigma if one of their members converts and, for this reason, the reaction of relatives is often much more severe than the reaction of outsiders. One interviewee said that a family's public image was a particularly crucial factor; converts may even be tolerated within the family until news of the conversion becomes widely known. Such social pressures are, of course, a far cry from the Western standards of acceptance and toleration, but, at the same time, persecution and shunning behaviors are more modest than the level of social persecution experienced by Muslim converts elsewhere.

The actions and attitudes of the Kurdish authorities are having a decisive impact on American missionary efforts to the region. As discussed above, Saddam's legacy of persecution partially explains the measure of religious tolerance afforded by the Kurdish Regional Government. The presence and power of the United States provides another partial explanation as it encourages the KRG to adhere to Western standards of human rights. These two factors are joined by a third key impetuous, namely economics.

Immediately after the Gulf War, economic conditions in the Kurdish areas of Iraq were bleak. The Anfal campaign had devastating consequences and Saddam was economically strangling the north. The newly formed KRG was politically fragile with little revenue or international recognition. It therefore had little choice but to welcome any and all foreign assistance.

During the inter-war period, conditions slightly improved. Oil smuggling provided a significant source of revenue and outside NGOs (including Christian groups) rebuilt houses, vaccinated livestock (which had been systematically denied vaccinations under Saddam), drilled water wells, tapped springs, and offered medical services. Kurdish tribal leaders expressed gratitude for the help, competed to receive assistance, and went so far as to protect foreign workers. One interviewee said the

Barzani tribe dispatched (without prior notice) a group of Kurds to guard their facilities. On another occasion, a tribal chief sacrificed a sheep for the protection of the NGO.

The economic incentive to welcome and cooperate with outsiders continued after 2003 and the Iraq War. The KRG has, thus far, maintained an open-door policy towards outside NGOs—a factor that allows Christian groups to operate within the area. Many interviewees attributed the KRG's openness to the economic benefits such groups bring.

The KRG has also directly assisted American missionary efforts to build schools and educational facilities. It gave two acres of land (valued at $2 million dollars) for the construction of the Baptist Cultural Center.[32] In similar fashion, the KRG has supported Servant Group International's efforts to build Christian schools. "Government officials have even granted land and assisted with construction of new school buildings in several cities."[33] Heather Mercer, the Executive Director of Global Hope, said Kurdish government officials have welcomed their efforts to construct the Freedom Center Iraq. "We have longstanding relationships with the local community and government officials, so they're very much for this work in their city."[34]

Most interviewees said that KRG officials are not unaware of the fact that some of the foreigners coming into Iraq are religiously motivated Christians. In fact, all Westerners are generally assumed to be Christians and this perception may make it difficult for Kurdish officials to clearly distinguish between "missionaries" and "Westerners." All are engaged in similar activities, e.g., relief and development work, even if some are more anxious to share their faith than others. In any event, an attitude of "plausible deniability" exists whereby evangelistic efforts by Christians are overlooked so long as they are not too overt or causing civil disturbances. For this reason, missionaries in Iraq have found it extremely important to share their faith subtly through personal relationships. Public sermons, the distribution of religious tracks, inflammatory language or other more aggressive techniques are not used.

Another key dynamic is the cost-benefit trade-off to having foreign workers in the country. Weak states with poor economies need foreign assistance much more so than strong states with growing economies. After the Gulf War, the Kurds were in desperate need for help and the benefits of foreign assistance easily outweighed the political or social consequences of having missionaries present within the country. Nearly two decades on, circumstances have changed. The KRG is stronger and more legitimized, and the economy is improving. Several interviewees felt the KRG would continually re-evaluate the costs and benefits of foreign workers and allow them to remain only as long as it was politically expedient.

Summary

American Protestant missionary efforts to Iraqi Kurds have been deeply intertwined with the politics of the region. The U.S. intervention into Iraq during the Gulf War opened the door to mission-minded individuals and organizations for the first time in thirty years. U.S. government aid grants and protection further served as an inadvertent catalyst for mission groups. Mission efforts were halted temporarily following the U.S. withdrawal in 1996, but then recommenced following the Iraq War.

Saddam Hussein ineffectively tried to prevent foreign workers from operating in Northern Iraq. His Anfal campaign created an opportunity for missionaries by fostering discontent with Islam and a Kurdish social identity rooted more in ethnicity than religion. This paved the way for a modicum of religious toleration and acceptance of Kurdish converts.

The Kurdish Regional Government, moreover, has allowed American mission groups to operate in the region because of the economic benefits they provide and, in some cases, even materially supported their efforts. Economic conditions were bleak following the Gulf War; foreign assistance was desperately needed and welcomed. Even after the Iraq War, when the economy was relatively stronger, the KRG has encouraged foreign humanitarian groups, including Christian ones, to conduct operations in the region. Having analyzed the relationship between international politics and contemporary mission work among Iraqi Kurds, I will now present my second case study on mission efforts to Iranians.

---

[1] Robert Blincoe, *Ethnic Realities and the Church: Lessons from Kurdistan* (Pasadena: Presbyterian Center for Mission Studies, 1998), 78.

[2] Ibid., 40.

[3] Ibid., 169.

[4] Global Security.org, "Operation Provide Comfort," http://www.globalsecurity.org/ military/ops/provide_comfort.htm (accessed February 27, 2012).

[5] Robert Blincoe, Telephone Interview, Dallas TX, March, 2010.

[6] Tom Coburn, June 10, 2010, e-mail message to author.

[7] Kevin Fedarko, "Saddam's CIA Coup," *Time Magazine* (June 24th, 2001). http://www.time.com/time/magazine/article/0,9171,136540,00.html (accessed February 27, 2012).

[8] Thomas Goltz, "U.S. Quietly Abandons the Kurds of Northern Iraq," *L.A. Times* (December 29th, 2001). http://articles.latimes.com/1996-12-29/opinion/op-13478_1_northern-iraq (accessed Febuary 27, 2012).

[9] Michiel Leezenberg, "Humanitarian Aid in Iraqi Kurdistan," *CEMOTI.* no. 29 (2000): 31-49.

[10] Blincoe, Telephone Interview.

[11] U.S. Department of Defense, Office of the Assistant Secretary of Defense (Public Affairs), "Operation Pacific Haven Wraps Up Humanitarian Efforts," (April 15, 1997). http://www.defense.gov/releases/release.aspx?releaseid=1218 (accessed February 27, 2012).

[12] Michael G. Lortz, Willing to Face Death:A History of Kurdish Military Forces – the Peshmerga –from the Ottoman Empire to Present-Day Iraq (MA Thesis, Florida State University, 2005). 66-68.

[13] The figure is based on estimates made by multiple interviewees.

[14] Classical School of the Medes, "Welcome," http://csmedes.org/index.html (accessed February, 27 2012).

[15] Global Hope, "The Freedom Center," http://www.freedomcenteriraq.org/index.php?option=com_content&view=article&id=14&Itemid=11 (accessed February, 27 2012).

[16] Joni B. Hannigan, "Baptists in Iraqi's Kurdistan mark historic milestone for Christians," *Florida Baptist Witness,* October 13, 2011. http://www.gofbw.com/news.asp?ID=13383&fp=Y (accessed February 27, 2012).

[17] Blincoe, Telephone Interview.

[18] Based on various estimates made by interviewees.

[19] Conscience International, "The Gulf War and Beyond C I Sends Hands-On Aid to Refugees," http://conscienceinternational.wordpress.com/our-work/iraq/ (accessed February 27, 2012).

[20] Jody Veenker, "Iraq: Sanctions Missing the Mark," *Christianity Today*, June 12, 2000. http://www.christianitytoday.com/ct/article_print.html?id=15685 (accessed February 27, 2012).

[21] "U.S. Contingent Lands in Iraq to Deliver Aid," *Los Angeles Times*, January 14, 2001, http://articles.latimes.com/2001/jan/14/news/mn-12260 (accessed February 27, 2012).

[22] Common Dreams Progressive Newswire, "Americans Plan 'Walk for Peace' Across Iraqi Desert," May 16, 2002. http://www.commondreams.org/news2002/0516-13.htm (accessed February 27, 2012).

[23] Nashville Public Television, "Next Door Neighbors: Little Kurdistan, Four Waves of Resettlement," http://www.wnpt.org/productions/nextdoorneighbors/kurds/fourwaves.html (accessed February 27, 2012).

[24] U.S. Congress, *Congressional Record*, 1995, 104th Cong. 1st sess., Vol. 280, 149.

[25] Kurdistan –The Other Iraq, "Adverts from The Other Iraq Campaign 2006," http://www.theotheriraq.com/index.html (accessed February 27, 2012).

[26] The Other Iraq Tours, "About Us," http://www.theotheriraqtours.com/about (accessed February 27, 2012).

[27] Goltz, "U.S. Quietly Abandons," 2001.

[28] Michiel Leezenberg, "The Anfal Operation in Iraqi Kurdistan," *Century of Genocide, 3rd ed.* Ed. Samuel Totten and William S. Parsons. (New York: Routledge, 2009), 461-465.

[29] Ibid.

[30] Christine Gosden, "Why I Went, What I Saw," *Washington Post*, March 11, 1998. http://www.krg.org/articles/print.asp?anr=57&lngnr=12&rnr=223 (accessed February 27, 2012).

[31] Nechirvan Barzani, "PM's speech at inter-faith religious leaders' conference," February 17, 2009. http://www.krg.org/articles/detail.asp?lngnr=12&smap=02040100&rnr=268&anr=28005 (accessed February 27, 2012).

[32] Joni B. Hannigan, "Baptist in Iraqi's Kurdistan."

[33] Classical School of the Medes, "Welcome."

[34] Erin Roach, "'Cry for freedom' unfolding in the Middle East, Mercer says," *Baptist Press,* (May 9, 2011).

Chapter 4: Case Study on Iran

Iran was a focus of first wave missionary efforts to the Middle East. In 1805 Henry Martyn, a British missionary, traveled to Iran and translated the New Testament into Farsi. He died before the translation was published, but the work paved the way for later mission efforts.[1]

In 1830 Eli Smith and H. G. O. Dwight, two of the ABCFM's earliest missionaries to the Middle East, visited Assyrian Christians in the city of Urmia and reported, "We have found a field ripe for the harvest." Smith personally "felt a stronger desire to settle among them at once as a missionary than among any people I have seen."[2] The board subsequently dispatched Justin Perkins in 1832 to be the first permanent American missionary to Iran. For the next 100 years, Presbyterian missionaries expended considerable effort to evangelize and revitalize the Assyrian Christians in Northern Iran.[3]

American missionaries initially enjoyed good relations with the Assyrian churches. The Assyrians welcomed the missionaries and participated in their teaching and translating work. The Assyrian clergy regularly invited the missionaries to preach in their churches; mission schools were filled with Assyrian students.[4] Under Perkins' leadership, the missionaries worked in cooperation with the Assyrians rather than by establishing independent Protestant churches.[5] Conversely, the missionaries working among Maronite and Armenian Christians in the Ottoman Empire had a very strained relationship; the Maronite Patriarch pronounced anathema on all Protestant missionaries and their converts in 1832; the Armenian Patriarch followed suit in 1846. First wave missionaries in Iran also had relatively good relations with the Iranian government. The ruling Qajar Dynasty welcomed missionaries and associated their efforts with modernization; a Qajar Prince even donated money to the mission station.[6]

The Iranian mission field did not remain favorable in the long run. After Perkins returned to the U.S. in 1869, relations with the Assyrian church worsened and American missionaries began establishing independent Protestant churches.[7] Moreover, World War I wiped out mission work in Urmia and heightened tensions between Iranian Christians and Muslims. The conflict tarnished the reputation of American missionaries because they had participated in the hostilities.

After World War I, the Presbyterians slowly re-established their presence in Northern Iran. By 1922, they had reached a new peak with 92 missionaries in the country, but they soon encountered new challenges.[8] In 1925, Reza Shah overthrew the Qajar Dynasty and established the new, Pahlavi Dynasty. Although the missionaries welcomed his ascent, he soon moved to curtail mission work.[9]

The centerpiece of Presbyterian mission work was a chain of schools established with the intent of civilizing and Christianizing the local population. The new government quickly asserted control over them. In 1927, it ordered that the Koran be taught in all schools; in 1928 it restricted the use of Christian literature in schools; in 1930, praying and singing hymns in schools was forbidden; in 1932, Iranians were prohibited from attending missionary schools. By the end of the 1930s, all of the schools were nationalized and brought under the direct control of the Iranian government. In 1934, the missionaries were also forced to abandon their presence in Urmia—the long time seat of American mission effort. During this timeframe, the local Protestant congregations also became independent from the American Presbyterian church.

Despite these setbacks, Presbyterian efforts to Iran continued after World War II and other denominations and organizations became active there as well. The Assemblies of God began establishing churches during the 1960s.[10] The Southern Baptists dispatched their first missionary to Iran in 1967.[11] Campus Crusade for Christ established its Middle East headquarters in Tehran in 1975.[12] By 1979, there were an estimated 100 American Protestant missionaries.[13] Yet their efforts bore few converts. "The missionaries failed in converting

Persians."[14] In 1979, nearly 150 years after the arrival of the first American missionary to Iran, there were roughly 3,000 Protestants there (drawn mostly from Assyrian and Armenian Christians) including 300 Muslim converts.[15] By comparison, the BFMPC reported having nearly 3,000 communicants there prior to World War I.[16]

The Iranian Revolution again dramatically changed the mission field. Most of the American missionaries voluntarily left during the revolution. A few returned, but the new government soon forced them to permanently leave.[17] The Islamist regime also began persecuting Protestant Christians with increasing severity to the point that, by 1993, it adopted a policy of "gradual eradication of existing churches under legal pretenses."[18]

Ironically, 1993 also marked the beginning of another change within Iran that would dramatically alter the mission landscape. That year, at the 6th International Book Festival in Tehran, large crowds saw, for the first time, international TV channels freely available with a satellite TV dish. Demand for service was strong and by 1995 there were an estimated 500,000 satellite-dish-receivers in Tehran alone.[19] At the time, virtually none of the programming was in Farsi.

The proliferation of satellite-TV dishes caused consternation within the government. In 1994 the Interior Ministry declared (without legal authority) that satellite dishes were illegal. The move led to lengthy internal political debates over how to deal with the popular medium and culminated with the prohibition of satellite TV in 1995.[20] Nevertheless, adoption continued and by 2011 one-half of all Iranians were watching satellite TV.[21] A 2012 survey found one-in-four households had a satellite TV dish.[22] In an ironic mix of policies, the government itself began airing programming via the same satellites.[23]

In 1996 the Voice of America began broadcasting a weekly, Farsi-language program that triggered considerable controversy. The broadcast included tips on how to immigrate to the United States and played music from popular Iranian musicians that were considered decadent by the Iranian government. The response was a renewed crack-down on satellite TV dishes. To the further consternation of the government, Iranian exiles in California began broadcasting Farsi-language programming in 2000.[24]

In 2002 Sat-7, a U.S. based, satellite TV ministry to the Middle East, began broadcasting Farsi-language Christian programming. There were only two hours of programming initially offered on a channel that otherwise featured Arabic-language content. Nevertheless, the amount of programming steadily increased and other American ministries began producing and broadcasting content as well. In 2006 Sat-7 launched a separate channel dedicated to Farsi-language programming; by 2012 there were four Christian channels broadcasting 24 hours per day.[25]

Christian satellite TV broadcasts followed precedents set by Christian radio ministries. Even prior to the revolution, Voice of Christ Media Ministries (then part of Christar, an American mission organization) had been broadcasting radio programming into Iran using short-wave frequencies. Trans World Radio similarly began broadcasting via short-wave radio in the 1980s, shortly after the revolution.

Christian TV and radio programming features a mix of English-language shows dubbed into Farsi as well as Farsi-language programs produced specifically for the Middle East. Programming seeks to attract a wide range of audiences ranging from children to adults, non-Christians as well as Christians.

Mission organizations complement broadcasts with online efforts and call centers which encourage viewers to connect with them by telephone, email, Facebook, websites and chat-rooms. They report a warm reception from their viewers. Iran Alive Ministries, for example, says it has received over 100,000 calls from Iran since 2001 and 10,000 unique visitors to its website.[26] Interviewees similarly report that the larger organizations receive 100s of calls each month and that Iranians contact mission organizations to ask questions about Christianity, solicit personal advice, or share stories about their faith and experiences. Mission organizations maintain ongoing communication with a small number of converts in Iran.

Mission organizations report that Protestant Christianity is growing in Iran.[27] Iran Alive Ministries says it has documented 22,318 conversions since it began broadcasting in 2001.[28] Iranian Christian International reports there are 25,000 converts in Iran.[29] Elam Ministries and Operation World (both Christian organizations) claim there are a total 100,000 converts.[30] A book published by Voice of the Martyrs, (a Christian organization dedicated to combating persecution) called the growth of Protestant Christianity in Iran "the fastest growing Muslim movement in the world."[31] One interviewee estimated there were 100,000 Christian converts in Iran as well as many others that convert for a time, but then eventually abandon their new faith.[32]

Independent entities, although less sanguine, also report that Protestant Christianity is growing in Iran. A report by the Norwegian government concluded:

> There are no reliable figures available on the number of converts living in Iran. Reliable statistics do not exist, and figures presented by various sources cannot be verified because of the circumstances prevailing in the country. Nor is it possible to establish whether the number of converts in Iran is increasing. However, in the opinion of Landinfo, the source material, on which this report is based, indicates a tendency towards growth in the volume of house churches during recent years.

The report went on to cite figures from various sources ranging from 5,000 to 1,000,000.[33]

Broadcasts appear to play a key role in the growth of Protestant Christianity in Iran. One interviewee said the role of media was of "paramount importance."[34] Religion scholar Christian Van Gorder concluded, "There is some evidence that such evangelistic radio programs beamed into Iran have resulted in Muslims converting to Christianity."[35] The aforementioned

Norwegian government report noted house-church meetings sometimes center on Christian programs broadcast via satellite. Stefan De Groot, a mission worker with Open Doors said, "New media is becoming increasingly important in the future to strengthen the church." "The majority of people now come to faith through the multimedia, and especially satellite TV. Nobody can control which programs Iranians watch."[36] *U.S. News and World Report* similarly called attention to the role of satellite TV programs, interviewing an Iranian Muslim family that secretly converted to Christianity after watching broadcasts.[37]

Missionaries evangelizing Iran often place their efforts within the context of Biblical prophecies concerning Elam—an ancient, pre-Islamic civilization that was located in Western Iran.[38] In the Book of Jeremiah, God decrees disaster for Elam but also promises a resurrection:

> This is the word of the Lord that came to Jeremiah the prophet concerning Elam, early in the reign of Zedekiah king of Judah:
>
> This is what the Lord Almighty says:
>
> "See, I will break the bow of Elam, the mainstay of their might.
>
> I will bring against Elam the four winds from the four quarters of heaven;
>
> I will scatter them to the four winds, and there will not be a nation where Elam's exiles do not go.
>
> I will shatter Elam before their foes, before those who want to kill them;

I will bring disaster on them, even my fierce anger," declares the Lord.

"I will pursue them with the sword until I have made an end of them.

I will set my throne in Elam and destroy her king and officials," declares the Lord.

"Yet I will restore the fortunes of Elam in days to come," declares the Lord.[39]

Many of the missionaries evangelizing Iran believe this passage predicts the Christianization of contemporary Iran. Reza Safa, provides an illustrative example. Safa founded Nejat TV which broadcasts into Iran in partnership with the Trinity Broadcast Network, the world's largest religious network. In his book, *The Coming Fall of Islam in Iran,* Safa discusses the above passage and its implications:

> Note verse 38: "'I will set my throne in Elam, and will destroy from there the king and the princes,' says the Lord." Isn't this what is happening in Iran right now? Did we see it? And do we see it now? God is working one of the most awesome moves that has ever taken place on this planet, and yet most of the church world doesn't even know. For the first time in the history of an Islamic nation, thousands upon thousands of Muslims are converting to Christ. This is a phenomenal miracle. God is pouring out His Spirit in Iran, and the faith of the gospel is being established in the hearts of the Iranian populace for the first time in their history. God is establishing His throne in a radical Islamic nation. Iran is becoming a prototype of the fall of Islam in the hearts of millions of ex-Muslims. This is amazing and glorious! I believe that within the next few years millions of Iranians

will become strong Christians and great witnesses for Jesus in the Muslim world.[40]

Safa goes on to say, "Iran has been a key nation in God's plan in times past, and I believe that God will use Iran today, again for His plan of salvation for the Muslim world. I believe that Iran is the axe that God will put to the tree of Islam to break the strength of Islam in the Muslim world."[41]

Other missionaries have expressed similar sentiments. Elam Ministries derives its name from the above passage. Iran Alive Ministries states on its website, "Our vision is to 'Transform Iran into a Christian Nation, in this Generation', according to Jeremiah 49:38 – 'I will set my throne in Elam,' declares the LORD."[42] Some interviewees privately echo this view and interpret these passages as a prophecy that Iran will become a Christian nation. At the same time, they interpret other passages as prophecies that Iran will militarily attack Israel.[43] When asked why Iran, as a Christian nation, would attack Israel, the response of multiple interviewees was that the Iranian population would become Christian, but the Iranian government would remain Islamic. Scholarly work has also documented the connection between Iranian mission work and Jeremiah Chapter 49. Political scientist Kathryn Spellman interviewed representatives of American and British mission organizations as part of her research:

> I asked several informants to explain the significance of the passage cited above. The most frequent response was

that millions of Persian speakers will respond to God's Gospel and restore the fortunes of the Elamites.[44]

Such interpretations theologically distinguish mission efforts to Iran from other Middle Eastern countries and, in some ways, are similar to the post-millennial expectations held by missionaries a century earlier. First wave missionaries anticipated rapid growth of Christianity in the region because of their post-millennial interpretations of Biblical prophecy; some second wave missionaries anticipate rapid growth in Iran on the basis of Jeremiah Chapter 49. Curiously, Iran Alive Ministries borrows (perhaps unintentionally) a phrase from the SVM rallying cry and declares a goal of reaching Iran in "this generation." [45]

Impact of Mission Work on International Politics

American mission efforts to Iran appear to have little political influence. Interviewees report that mission organizations generally avoid expressing political views on their broadcasts for fear it will undermine evangelistic efforts. Mission organizations do not want to be associated with the U.S. government or groups opposed to the Iranian government. One interviewee said that, in 2009, when Iranian protesters clashed with the government over election results, the mission organization he worked for encouraged Iranians to peacefully submit to government authority.[46] Another stated that the ministry he worked for supported Israel and was consequently branded by many in Iran as a "Zionist" organization.[47]

Mission organizations are hesitant to advocate for Christians in Iran. Interviewees said advocacy efforts can worsen the plight of Iranian Christians by associating them with Western ministries. Nevertheless, mission organizations will occasionally call attention to Christians that have been arrested through newsletters or broadcasts. One interviewee said his organization only publically advocated for Iranian Christians once they were sentenced to be executed; in such cases they felt there was little to lose through advocacy efforts.[48]

The growth of Protestant Christianity in Iran also does not appear to be having any political implications, at present. The presence of a growing Christian population naturally challenges the government's efforts to Islamize society. A Danish report claimed, "The growing number of conversions (the number is growing, however, the group remains relatively small) is considered a serious problem by the authorities."[49] Yet the number of converts, even by more generous estimates, is tiny as a portion of all Iranians. Operation World's figure of 100,000 converts amounts to 0.1% of the total population.

Impact of International Politics on Mission Work

International politics has had a tremendous impact on mission work in Iran. For one, it largely shaped the missionary presence in Iran. The Qajar Dynasty welcomed American missionaries and allowed them to establish local churches, hospitals, and schools. Between 1830 and 1914, American missionaries established an impressive network of schools as well as a modest number of Protestant churches.[50] World War I interrupted mission work in Western Iran and wiped out the missionary presence in Urmia—the seat of American mission efforts to the country. The rise of the Pahlavi Dynasty in 1925 further dismantled mission work by restricting educational efforts, nationalizing mission schools, and prohibiting missionaries from working in Urmia. The Iranian Revolution in 1979 ended the American missionary presence in Iran. American missionaries were forced to leave the country and they have only been permitted back on select occasions.[51] These events, in turn, led the missionaries to shift their strategy and rely heavily on satellite and radio broadcasts rather than a local presence.

The Iranian Revolution also impacted mission work by severely restricting religious freedom in the country and actively persecuting Christians. The Ayatollah Khomeini referred to religious minorities as "traitors" and "economic plunderers." The new government initially tolerated Presbyterian and Pentecostal congregations because they were financially and organizationally independent from the American churches that formed them. It targeted Anglican congregations, on the other hand, because they were still financially supported by churches in Britain. By the end of the campaign, the Anglican Church in Iran was left without any priests and church services had been driven underground. Notably, the Pahlavi government had also singled out Anglican churches; it restricted their ability to publish church literature and monitored its activities through SAVAK, the Iranian secret police.[52]

By the 1990s, the Iranian government had adopted its policy of "gradual eradication of existing churches under legal pretences" and was targeting Christians of all denominations.[53] The government closed churches, confiscated Bibles and Christian literature, and arrested, tortured and assassinated Church leaders. It also threatened Iranian lay Protestants with imprisonment or death if they evangelized Muslims.[54] In 1993, the same year of the new policy, tensions between the government and Protestants came to a head. In December of 1993 Mehdi Dibaj, a pastor and Muslim convert to Christianity, was sentenced to death for apostasy. Haik Hovsepian-Mehr, a pastor at an Iranian Assembly of God church and the chairman of the Council of Protestant Ministers, publically campaigned for his release. Under growing international pressure, the Iranian government relented and freed Dibaj but, three days later, Haik was found dead. Six months later, Dibaj disappeared only to be found dead; Tateos Michaelian, Haik's successor on the Protestant Council of Ministers was also murdered around the same time.[55]

The Iranian government continued to restrict evangelistic activities during the 2000s. The U.S. State Department's 2010 International Religious Freedom Report on Iran stated:

Proselytizing of Muslims by non-Muslims is illegal. Evangelical church leaders were subjected to pressure from authorities to sign pledges that they would not evangelize Muslims or allow Muslims to attend church services.

Christians of all denominations reported the presence of security cameras outside their churches allegedly to confirm that no non-Christians participate in services.

The government enforced its prohibition on proselytizing by closely monitoring the activities of evangelical Christians, discouraging Muslims from entering church premises, closing churches, and arresting Christian converts... The government restricted meetings for evangelical services to Sundays, and church officials were ordered to inform the Ministry of Information and Islamic Guidance before admitting new members. [56]

Muslims who convert to Christianity and Christians that attempt to evangelize Muslims face draconian (albeit inconsistently enforced) punishments. In 1999, the Iranian Penal Code was revised so that apostasy, which can include conversion to a non-Muslim religion, is punishable by death. A report from the Danish government found:

According to a Western embassy, punishment for conversion is not practiced and does not take place. However, other sources consulted did not agree with this statement and according to the Attorney at Law, the punishment for conversion is the death penalty. He explained that if a private person accuses someone of conversion the government must intervene and a prosecutor will then pursue the private complaint. At this stage of prosecution, the person who made the complaint cannot withdraw it. It is up to the judge how to rule in the case of conversion.[57]

The Iranian government attempts to block American mission efforts originating outside Iran, as well. Interviewees reported that the government jams satellite TV broadcasts, confiscates satellite dishes, firewalls mission websites, and taps or blocks phone calls to mission organizations. The Iranian government is also said to broadcast anti-Christian programming under the name of a known Christian mission organization—the apparent aim is to influence listeners seeking Christian programming.[58] One interviewee reported that members of the Iranian government telephoned death threats and branded the mission organization a "threat to their national security."[59] Another said the Iranian government sent agents to kill him while he was in Europe, but the plot failed.[60] The Iranian government's efforts to block Christian programming are part of a larger campaign to block satellite TV programming it finds objectionable. The U.S. government's Voice of America, the BBC News' Persian language channel and anti-government broadcasts from Iranian exiles are key targets of the campaign.[61] Mission organizations, for their part, employ technological techniques to counter the government's efforts. Broadcast frequencies are altered, phone numbers are changed, and proxy servers are used to circumvent firewalls. Repeat broadcast of programming also helps Iranians to view blocked programs. Jamming efforts are reportedly less successful late at night and Iranians simply record broadcasts for later viewing.

Migration scholar Sebnem Koser Akcapar has researched yet another area in which international politics is having an impact on mission work. Her work, which focused on Iranian asylum-seekers in Turkey, concluded:

> Conversion is also used as a migration strategy. Apostasy is a crime in Iran, and because converts may be subject to death, they cannot be deported back to Iran under the principle of non-refoulement, which Turkey has started to apply to harmonize its own immigration policies with those of the European Union.[62]

Interviewees confirmed that Iranians sometimes convert in an effort to migrate from Iran. (When asked about the issue, one interviewee notably said that he himself had originally converted for that reason but later became a sincere convert and active missionary.)[63] A Danish fact-finding mission to Iran further documented the phenomenon. A Christian church in Tehran reported to the mission that conversion was indeed seen as a migration strategy:

> The source explained that a great number of young people wish to be able to certify that they have converted in order to go to the West, since they believe that conversion makes it easier to be granted asylum abroad. "Nowadays, young Muslim people feel under pressure and they feel that if they go to any church and are baptized, then they might have relief and find a way out of Iran." The source did not consider that everyone is sincere when asking for the blessing of a Christian ministry and considered it "conversion for convenience."[64]

At the same time, the report pointed to evidence that migration is not the reason for conversion in most cases:

A Western embassy considered that conversion is not the main reason why Iranians apply for asylum abroad. However, the embassy stated that the converts they have been in contact with do not use conversion as an "easy way" to the West. [sic] The embassy added that it may see around 10 asylum cases of converts a year. The embassy was aware of these cases, as it has been requested to verify the documents that Iranian converts present to the asylum authorities. [65]

The most profound way international politics is impacting mission work in Iran is the unintended consequence of having rigorous government policies designed to promote Islam. Contrary to intentions, such policies are actually greatly *encouraging* conversion to Christianity by fostering resentment against Islam. Multiple scholars have noted this dynamic. Sociologist Kathryn Spellman observed it in her work:

> People were increasingly becoming disillusioned with what the Islamic Revolution had brought them. My contacts (who converted to Christianity in Iran and are now members of the Iranian church in London) said they felt both trapped by the Islamic rules that were being forcibly implemented by the police and defenseless, with no space to mobilize against the state's policies. Many said that before the revolution they identified themselves as Muslims and participated in some religious traditions, but they did not regularly say their prayers everyday or follow all the dietary laws. Many stated that they became increasingly disillusioned with Islam when the Islamic regime started to force people to practice its faith. It was then that many of my contacts formed the opinion that Islam is a harsh religion, with a degenerative effect on society… more Iranians than ever before became receptive to Christianity.[66]

For example, one of her interviewees stated, "After the revolution, we had to learn about Islam, whether we liked it or not. Seeing what the Islamic government did to my country has put me off Islam forever."[67] Spellman concludes that the rise of the Islamic Revolution has substantially benefited the missionary enterprise: "Since the revolution, evangelical Christian missionaries have been successful for the first time in converting a number of Iranians from Muslim backgrounds, living both inside and outside Iran, to Christianity."[68] Akcapar's interviews of Iranian Christian converts also documented the phenomenon. She noted, "All the interviewees in Turkey, regardless of their time and place of conversion, underlined the distance between the use of religion in Iran and the people." One of her interviewees stated, "The regime made us hate Islam."[69]

In addition to academic scholars, the missionaries themselves frequently point to a connection between the repressive policies of the Islamic Republic and the growing number of Christian converts. Reza Safa has stated,

> The turning point in the history of the church in Iran and among Iranians was the Islamic Revolution of 1979. The implementation of Islamic law has led to this phenomenal thirst and to an unprecedented exodus from the Muslim faith. The openness of Iranians to the gospel is primarily due to the oppression they have suffered at the hands of the Islamic clergymen who rule the nation with an ironfisted regime. Tens of thousands of former Shiite Muslims are now Bible-believing Christians.[70]

Many interviewees expressed similar sentiments. During two separate interviews, the Ayatollah Khomeini was called, tongue in cheek, the "greatest evangelist" for Christianity because his policies drove people away from Islam.[71] Interviewees spoke of the Iranian Revolutions exposing "the real face of Islam."[72] Another reported that their broadcast ministry (which had been active prior to 1979) witnessed a strong increase in responses a few years after the revolution.[73] Several interviewees also perceive a historical parallel—Islam, per their view, had originally been forced onto Iranians by Arabs and was now being forced on Iranians by small group of fanatical clerics.

Summary

The case of contemporary Iran is a case of extremes. The extremist, Islamist policies that followed the Iranian Revolution have had a tremendous impact on American Protestant mission work. Ironically, the policies have both hindered and helped American mission work. The Islamist government of Iran explicitly set a policy of preventing mission work and eradicating Christianity. It has expended considerable effort to that end: American missionaries are not allowed into the country; the broadcasts, websites, and telephone numbers of American mission organizations are blocked; Iranians that convert to Christianity are threatened with death and imprisonment. And yet at the same time, the government's oppressive Islamist policies have fostered a rejection of Islam and openness to

Christianity. The Islamic Republic of Iran thus (in a sense) made attainable a goal that eluded American missionaries for over a century: the conversion of a significant number of Muslims to Christianity.

While political factors are having a tremendous impact on mission work, mission work is having little political impact. In large part, this is because mission organizations no longer have a presence in Iran. There are no mission stations to become an interest of U.S. foreign policy and no Americans in need of representation or protection by the U.S. government. Similarly, there are no longer any mission schools to become hubs of political activism. Without a significant presence inside the country, American mission organizations can only influence politics from afar by way of advocacy work or their broadcasts. Yet even these two channels are seldom used. Mission organizations are hesitant to engage in advocacy work because they understand advocacy efforts can endanger Iranian Christians by associating them with the U.S. They also avoid discussing political events in Iran for fear politicizing their mission message will undermine its evangelistic power.

To conclude, contemporary Iran presents a case where political factors are having an enormous influence on mission work and, on balance, a beneficial one despite the express intentions of the Iranian government. Iran is a rare example where a substantive number of Muslims allegedly are converting to Christianity. The significance of the occurrence should not be missed. American Protestants have been trying to convert Muslims in the Middle East for nearly two-hundred years without success. If these reports prove true, the phenomenon is a reality in Iran today. It would be all the more notable that political factors are yielding such an unprecedented result at a time when mission work is at a nadir of political influence. Never before have American missionary efforts appeared to be more successful; never before have they had less political influence in Iran. Having analyzed the relationship between international politics and contemporary mission work to Iranians, I will now present a third case study on the Palestinians.

---

[1] Mansoori, "American Missionaries," 30.

[2] Ibid., 31-32.

[3] The Presbyterians initially operated within the ABCFM but then formed their own board, the BFMPC, in 1837. The Persian mission was transferred to the new entity in 1870. By common consent, the American Presbyterians focused their efforts on Northern Iran while British Anglicans focused their efforts on Southern Iran.

[4] Heleen Murre-van den Berg, "The American Board and the Eastern Churches: the 'Nestorian Mission' (1844-1846)," *Orientalia Christiana Periodica* 65, no. 1 (1999): 119.

[5] Ultimately, the missionaries did establish independent Protestant churches but not until 1870, after Perkins had died.

[6] Mansoori, "American Missionaries," 42-43.

Kathryn Spellman, Religion and Nation: Iranian Local and Transnational Networks in Britain, (New York: Bergham Books, 2004), 158-159.

[7] Murre-van den Berg, "Nestorian Mission," 137.

[8] The number of schools and churches, however, never recovered from the pre-World War I peak; BFMPC. *1922 Annual Report,* (New York: BFMPC, 1922), 435, 443.

[9] Zirinsky, "Render Therefore Unto Caesar."

[10] AOG efforts actually began in the 1920s but increased substantially in the 1960s; Christian A. Van Gorder, Christianity in Persia and the Status of

Non-Muslims in Modern Iran, (Lanham: Lexington Books, 2010), 145-146; Spellman, Religion and Nation, 162.

[11] Van Gorder, *Christianity in Persia*, 148; Southeastern Baptist Theological Seminary, "Oral History Interview with Dr. George W. Braswell, Jr.," Southeastern SBC Historical Missiology Oral History Program (November 28, 2005).

[12] Iranian Christians International, "Iranian Evangelical Christians – Some Sociological and Demographic Information," 4 http://www.asylumlaw.org/docs/iran/IRN_3/SEC%20II/Iranian%20Evangelical.pdf (accessed July 27, 2012).

[13] Telephone interview with individual involved in mission work in the Middle East, Dallas, TX, June 22, 2012.

[14] Mansoori, "American Missionaries," 159.

[15] Iranian Christians International, "Iranian Evangelical Christians," 6.

[16] BFMPC, *1914 Annual Report*, 334, 348.

[17] Notably, some American missionaries returned to Iran after the revolution but were soon forced to leave by the new government; Telephone interview with individual involved in mission work in the Middle East, Dallas, TX, June 22, 2012.

[18] Spellman, *Religion and Nation*, 167.

[19] Steven Barraclough, "Satellite Television in Iran: Prohibition, Imitation and Reform," *Middle Eastern Studies* 37, no. 3 (July., 2001): 30.

[20] Ibid., 31-33.

[21] Paul Sonne and Farnaz Fassihi, "In Skies Over Iran, a Battle for Control of Satellite TV," *The Wall Street Journal* (December 27, 2011) http://online.wsj.com/article/SB10001424052970203501304577088380199787036.html (accessed July 27, 2012).

[22] Broadcasting Board of Governors, "BBG Research Series Briefing: Iran Media Use 2012," June 12, 2012 http://www.bbg.gov/wp-content/media/2012/06/BBG-Iran-ppt.pdf (accessed July 27, 2012.

[23] Ibid.

[24] The exiles notably included many Iranian celebrities that were popular in Iran prior to the revolution but forced out by the Iranian government. Programming quickly took on a strong, anti-government flavor; Barraclough, "Satellite Television in Iran," 34; Michael Lewis, "The Satellite Subversives," *The New York Times,* (February 24, 2002), http://www.nytimes.com/2002/02/24/magazine/ 24NITV.html?pagewanted=all (accessed July 27, 2012).

[25] Farsi-language channels include Sat-7 PARS, Iran Alive Ministries' Network 7, Mohabat TV, and TBN Nejat TV.

[26] Iran Alive Ministries, "Track Record" http://www.iranaliveministries.org/page.aspx? n=16&s=20121323111349&p=Our%20Track%20Record (accessed July 27, 2012).

[27] Mission organizations, of course, have a desire and also a self-interest in seeing Muslim conversions. One interviewee said mission organizations exaggerate operational and conversion statistics in order to raise funds from domestic supporters. At the same time, the interviewee also said Protestant Christianity was growing in Iran; Telephone interview with individual involved in mission work in the Middle East, Dallas, TX, August 28, 2012.

[28] Ibid.

[29] Spellman, *Religion and Nation*, 166.

[30] Operation World, "Iran" http://www.operationworld.org/iran (accessed July 27, 2012); Norway, Country of Origin Information Center (Landinfo), *Report Iran: Christians and Converts*, (Oslo, July 7, 2011), 10.

[31] Voice of the Martyrs, *Iran: Desperate for God* (Bartlesville: Living Sacrifice Book Company, 2006), 12.

[32] Telephone interview with individual involved in mission work in the Middle East, DallasTX, August 28, 2012.

[33] Landinfo, *Iran: Christians and Converts*, 10-11.

[34] Email correspondence with individual involved in mission work in the Middle East, July 18, 2012.

[35] Van Gorder, *Christianity in Persia*, 149.

[36] Jennifer Riley, "Christianity Spreading in Iran via Multimedia," *Christian Today* (June 23, 2007). http://www.christiantoday.com/article/christianity.spreading.in.iran.via.multimedia/11248.htm (accessed August 10, 2012).

[37] Anuj Chopra, "In Iran, Covert Christian Converts Live With Secrecy and Fear," *U.S. News and World Report* (May 8, 2008). http://www.usnews.com/news/world/articles/2008/05/08/in-iran-covert-christian-converts-live-with-secrecy-and-fear (accessed July 27, 2012).

[38] History of the Elam civilization stretches between 3,200 and 539 B.C. Elam was subjugated by the Assyrian Empire during its later years and eventually incorporated into the Medio-Persian Empire in 539 B.C.

[39] Jeremiah 49:34-39 (NIV)

[40] Reza Safa, *The Coming Fall of Islam in Iran* (Lake Mary: FrontLine, 2006), 162.

[41] Ibid., 164.

[42] Iran Alive Ministries, "Vision," http://www.iranaliveministries.org/page.aspx? n=15&s=20121323111335&p=Our%20Vision (accessed July 27, 2012).

[43] This view draws on dispensational premillennial views of Biblical prophecies. See chapter four for more on this.

[44] Spellman, *Religion and Nation*, 148; It should be noted that not all missionaries evangelizing Iran hold such views. Spellmen interviewed one who said Jeremiah 49 had been taken out of context and should not be overemphasized. Similarly, some of my interviewees said Biblical prophecies regarding Elam were not relevant to contemporary Iran; Telephone interview with individual involved in mission work in the Middle East, Dallas, TX, July 9, 2012.

[45] Iran Alive Ministries, "Vision."

[46] Ibid.

[47] Telephone interview with individual involved in mission work in the Middle East, Dallas, TX, July 7, 2012.

[48] Ibid.

[49] Danish Refugee Council, *Human Rights Situation for Minorities, Women and Converts, end Entry and Exit Procedures, ID Cards, Summons and Reporting, etc. Fact finding mission to Iran 24th August – 2nd September 2008* (Copenhagen: April 2009), 31.

[50] By 1914, American missionaries had established 114 schools in Iran and 38 churches; BFMPC, *1914 Annual Report*, 334, 348.

[51] Following the Gulf War and the flood of Kurdish refugees into Turkey and Iran, a small group of American Baptists were allowed to provide relief services to Kurdish refugees in Iran. Similarly, after an earthquake hit the Iranian city of Bam in December of 2003, World Vision and other Christian relief organizations were allowed to distribute relief supplies and set up health clinics; Dick Hurst, *Religion, An Accident of Birth,* (Bloomington: Jones Harvest Publishing, 2008), 27-37; World Vision, "World Vision staff, relief aid slated for deadly Iran quake, (December 27, 2012). http://www.worldvision.org/worldvision/pr.nsf/stable/pr_iran_20031227 (accessed August 10, 2012).

[52] Spellman, *Religion and Nation*, 162-165.

[53] Ibid., 162-163.

[54] Ibid., 166-167.

[55] Ibid., 167-168.

[56] U.S. Department of State, *International Religious Freedom Report 2010: Iran,* September 13, 2011. http://www.state.gov/j/drl/rls/irf/2010_5/168264.htm (accessed July 27, 2012).

[57] Danish Refugee Council, *Human Rights Situation,* 30.

[58] Telephone interview with individual involved in mission work in the Middle East, Dallas, TX, August 28, 2012.

[59] Telephone interview with individual involved in mission work in the Middle East, Dallas, TX, July 7, 2012.

[60] Telephone interview with individual involved in mission work in the Middle East, Dallas, TX, August 28, 2012.

[61] Paul Sonne and Farnaz Fassihi, "In Skies Over Iran."; Michael Lewis, "The Satellite Subversives."

[62] Sebnem Koser Akcapar, "Conversion as a Migration Strategy in a Transit Country: Iranian Shiites Becoming Christians in Turkey," *International Migration Review* 40 no. 4 (Winter 2006):846.

[63] Interview with individual involved in mission work in the Middle East, Dallas, TX, July 9, 2012.

[64] Danish Refugee Council, *Human Rights Situation,* 32.

[65] Ibid., 33.

[66] Spellman, *Religion and Nation,* 165-166.

[67] Ibid., 183.

[68] Ibid., 198.

[69] Akcapar, "Conversion as a Migration Strategy," 835.

[70] Safa, *The Coming Fall of Islam in Iran,* 10.

[71] Telephone interview with individual involved in mission work in the Middle East, Dallas, TX, August 28, 2012; Interview with individual involved in mission work in the Middle East, Dallas, TX, November 1, 2011.

[72] Interview with individual involved in mission work in the Middle East, Dallas, TX, July 19, 2012; Telephone interview with individual involved in mission work in the Middle East, Dallas, TX, August 28, 2012.

[73] Telephone interview with individual involved in mission work in the Middle East, Dallas, TX, June 22, 2012.

Chapter 5: Case Study on Palestinians

American Protestant missionaries did not play a large role in Israel until after World War II. Pliny Fisk and Levi Parsons' were unsuccessful in evangelizing Jerusalem and in 1843 the ABCFM abandoned its presence there.[1] From 1851 to 1854, Dr. James T. Barclay worked in Jerusalem as the first appointee of the American Christian Missionary Society of the Disciples of Christ. He served there again from 1858-1862 and then briefly in 1865. The local population was unreceptive to his efforts, however, and he won few converts. His most notable achievement was his extensive studies into Biblical archeology and the publication of a lengthy work on the subject, *The City of the Great King*.[2]

Other denominations began sending missionaries to Israel/Palestine as the 20th century dawned. The Christian & Missionary Alliance and Assemblies of God established a presence shortly after their founding in 1887 and 1914, respectively. The Church of the Nazarene began operating in Jerusalem in 1921.[3] It was also during early 1900s that the

Southern Baptists, one of the nation's largest denominations, turned its attention to the region.

In 1896, the Southern Baptist Convention issued a resolution stating, "We regard as eminently important and desirable the establishment of a representative Baptist mission in Palestine."[4] Sukri Mussa, an Arab from a town north of the Sea of Galilee, realized this goal after becoming a Protestant Christian while studying in Texas.[5] Under the guidance of George W. Truett, pastor of the First Baptist Church of Dallas, and with the financial support of Baptist churches in Southern Illinois, Mussa returned in 1911 and began evangelizing. By 1926, a small group of converts had established the Nazareth Baptist Church. Mussa died in 1928 but in the 1930s, American Baptist missionaries arrived to build on his foundation. At one point, seven Baptist missionaries were present concurrently and they helped found additional Baptist churches as well as the Nazareth Baptist School in 1937. World War II interrupted mission work in the 1940s and forced missionaries to return home, temporarily closing the Nazareth Baptist School.[6]

Following World War II and the creation of the modern state of Israel, missionaries renewed their activities. The Nazareth Baptist School reopened; American Baptists pastored local churches and helped established more institutions including the George W. Truett Children's Home and the Baptist Village retreat center.[7] They also re-built the Ahli Arab Hospital in Gaza which had originally been built by British Anglican missionaries

in 1907 and was destroyed during World War I. Other
denominations also arrived after World War II. The Mennonite
Central Committee—the relief and development arm of the
Mennonite Church—came to Israel/Palestine after the 1948
Arab-Israeli War and the first Mennonite missionaries soon
followed. By the 1950s, the Brethren were likewise working in
the region.[8]

In the 1990s, the Southern Baptist mission board shifted
its strategic focus and stopped working directly with local Baptist
congregations. The Baptist legacy remains, however. The
Baptist Village continues to operate as a retreat center, there are
nearly 20 Baptist churches in Israel/Palestine, the Nazareth
Baptist School is one of the premier schools in Israel; and the
former home for Baptist missionaries is now the Nazareth
Evangelical Theological Seminary.[9]

Today, a variety of denominational and non-
denominational organizations work in Israel. Overt evangelism
efforts are socially shunned and organizations that seek converts
typically use subtle techniques. (Many interviewees stressed that
even the word "missionary" is a "dirty word" in Israel as the
word recalls European persecution.) The dominant method of
evangelizing is by slowly building relationships with non-
Christians and sharing religious views as opportunities arise.

Despite half a century of sustained effort, American
missionaries have had little success in converting Palestinians to
Protestant Christianity. There are only a small number of Arab

Protestant congregations in Palestine. Evangelicals comprise just 0.1% of the population and the percentage has precipitously fallen over the last fifty years as Palestinian Protestants immigrate to other countries to avoid the hardships of life in Palestine.[10]

Impact of Mission Work on International Politics

A small number of American missionaries have publically advocated for the Palestinians and criticized the Christian Zionist movement. For example, a group of Mennonite Christians working in Palestine presented theological arguments against Christian Zionism in the book *Under Vine and Fig Tree:*

> Mass dispossession and ethnic cleansing are universally condemned in contexts such as Rwanda, Sudan, or Bosnia. Christian Zionists readers of Scripture, however, implicitly (and sometimes explicitly) call for the removal of Palestinians from the land, a divinely mandated act of ethnic cleansing.[11]

Andrew Bush, a Professor of Missions at Eastern University who has worked with Palestinians since 1998, offered sharp criticisms of Christian Zionism in his article, *The Implications of Christian Zionism for Mission:*

> In condoning the use of force to achieve their missionary goals, Christian Zionism reveals a deep inconsistency. Throughout the world it seeks to advance the Gospel of the grace of God, with its forgiveness and mercy toward all people. Yet in the Middle East, without sense of contradiction, it advocates a theology of militarism to suppress a minority population, under the assumption that God blesses the disenfranchisement of the Palestinians.[12]

Thomas Gettman is another vocal advocate for the Palestinians. For five years, he served in Jerusalem as national director for World Vision—an evangelical relief and development organization. Gettman has offered some of the sharpest criticisms of Israel and Christian Zionism:

> Until the story of Palestinian suffering becomes part of the Jewish story, Israel will continue its slide into isolation and racism. And this is just as true for the church today, a church that has, tragically, through its theology, its silence, and its actions, supported the Jewish people's tragic yielding to the heresy that violence can redeem a people from suffering.[13]

Southern Baptist missionaries have influenced the political views expressed by their denomination. In 1982, the Southern Baptist Convention entertained a resolution expressing strong political support for Israel. After much debate, the measure was tabled because of opposition from R. Keith Parks, the head of the Southern Baptist Foreign Mission Board. Parks argued that the resolution would hinder mission work and "cause us to be identified politically in such a way that would jeopardize permits to work and safety of Baptists."[14] He also said there was "a difference regarding eschatology among board members and staff, as well as missionaries and Southern Baptists in general. None of us has a right to impose that personal conviction upon all Southern Baptists or to imply that all Southern Baptists hold to the conviction that any individual may hold."[15]

In 1984 a number of prominent Baptists including a former president of the Southern Baptist Convention, James

Draper, signed a statement of support for Israel which declared, "As Bible-believing Christian Americans, we reaffirm our absolute commitment to the welfare and security of the state of Israel and urge all Americans to demonstrate their solidarity with Israel."[16] In response, the board of trustees for the Foreign Mission Board issued a statement saying, "Our missionaries work with all Semitic people and they stress God's love for all people. They do not enter into the political debate of their countries and do not assume positions over one against another."[17]

While missionaries have occasionally criticized Israel, Christian Zionism or, in the case of the Southern Baptists, pressed for a more neutral policy stance, the Bethlehem Bible College (BBC) is one of the most interesting intersections of mission work and political influence. The non-denominational, Bethlehem Bible College was founded in 1979 by Bishara Awad—a naturalized-US citizen of Palestinian birth. Awad was raised by a mother who became a Christian through the influence of an American missionary.[18] He lived and studied in the United States for many years and then returned to Palestine in the 1970s to serve as the principal of a Christian secondary school that was founded by Mennonites. In the 1980s he received theological training from the Mennonite Brethren Biblical Seminary in Fresno, CA.[19]

Bishara Awad's background is similar to many others affiliated with the BBC. Jonathan Kuttab, the Chairman of BBC's board, is a Palestinian-born Christian and naturalized U.S.

citizen who received a law degree from the University of Virginia. Bishara's brother, Alex Awad, is also a member of the board, a naturalized U.S. citizen, and a missionary for the United Methodist Church.[20] Another board member, Labib Madanat, was born in Jerusalem and works with the American Bible Society. During much of the 1990s, Labib was a lay Pastor of a church originally founded by American missionaries—a position his father held 30 years previously.[21]

Board Members of the BBC have repeatedly advocated for Palestinians. Bishara Awad and Jonathan Kuttab are the Vice-Chairman and Chairman of Holy Land Trust, a Bethlehem-based non-profit which "through a commitment to the principles of nonviolence... seeks to strengthen and empower the Palestinian community in developing spiritual, pragmatic and strategic approaches that will allow it to resist all forms of oppression."[22] Kuttub has harshly criticized the Israeli occupation. "The behavior of the Jewish majority toward the Palestinian citizens of Israel has not been magnanimous or tolerant. Where ethnic cleansing was insufficient, military rule, land confiscation and systemic discrimination have all been employed."[23] He has also defended the role played by Arab Christians:

> Those who expect or accuse Arab Christians of siding with the West, and of being a "fifth column" for outsiders, have been consistently proven wrong. To the contrary, the unique position of Arab Christians, with their knowledge and understanding of the West has always been used to promote the interests of the Arab world and press for its

positions at every turn of the road. Even Christian institutions created by missionary funds and efforts, such as the American University of Beirut, turned out to be hot-beds of Arab nationalism and think tanks for creatively promoting the interests of the Arab world in confronting the West. Arab Christian institutions, such as schools, hospitals and non-governmental organizations, which are often funded by Christian churches in the West, continue in the same tradition to promote the interests of their people, especially in the face of invasion, occupation or aggression by the West.[24]

Alex Awad has called attention to the plight of the Palestinians. His book, *Through the Eyes of the Victims,* briefly chronicles the Palestinian perspective of the conflict and theologically challenges Christian Zionism. He has also called for Christians in the West to support Palestinian statehood:

> Western Christians who are concerned for the future of the Church in the Palestinian territories and the rest of the Middle East need to support the Palestinian drive for statehood… Christians tarnish their testimony in the world when they continue to endorse or be passive about the lingering injustice in Palestine.[25]

In 2010, the Bethlehem Bible College organized the *Christ at the Checkpoint* conference which sought to address the question, "How should Christ followers respond to this political, multi-faceted conflict?" The conference was supported by many leading American Christians including author Tony Campolo and Lynne Hybels, co-founder of Willow Creek Community Church—one of the largest churches in the U. S. The conference

drew together a notable collection of American evangelicals and
had four stated goals:

- Empower and encourage the Palestinian church.

- Expose the realities of the injustices in the Palestinian
  Territories and create awareness of the obstacles to
  reconciliation and peace.

- Create a platform for serious engagement with Christian
  Zionism and an open forum for ongoing dialogue between
  all positions within the Evangelical theological spectrum.

- Motivate participants to become advocates for the
  reconciliation work of the church in Palestine/Israel and
  its ramifications for the Middle East and the world.[26]

In line with these goals, speakers called attention to the plight of
Palestinians, called for peace and reconciliation in the region, and
challenged Christian Zionism. A second, follow-up conference
was held in 2012

The writings of Naim Ateek, a Palestinian Protestant
clergyman, theologically buttress the efforts of BBC board
members. Naim Ateek was exposed to Protestant Christianity at
a young age. His father, although raised in an Eastern Orthodox
Christian family, became an active Anglican under the influence
of British missionaries and helped found an Anglican
congregation in Beit She'an, Israel.[27] Naim Ateek attended the
Nazareth Baptist School and latter the Baptist-affiliated, Hardin-
Simmons University in Abilene, Texas. He earned a doctorate
from San Francisco Theological Seminary and became an

ordained Anglican priest serving as the Canon of St. George's Cathedral in Jerusalem.

When Ateek was a child, shortly after the State of Israel was proclaimed in 1948, the Israeli military forced his family to abandon their home. The military gave them only a few hours to pack and the family kept only possessions that they could carry. The Israeli government prohibited Palestinians from freely traveling within Israel and it was not until ten years later that Ateek's family was able to return to their former home. When they did, they found it occupied by a Jewish family who would not permit them to look inside. They were curtly told, "This is not your house; it is ours." Shortly after the visit, Ateek's father had a multiple strokes and became immobilized.[28]

The events left a lasting impression on Ateek and today he is the principal formulator and advocate for Palestinian Liberation Theology. In 1989, he published *Justice, and Only Justice* which presents a Biblical argument against Zionism. The story of Naboth recorded in 1 Kings provides a "central biblical paradigm" for his argument.[29] In this story, the wicked Jewish King Ahab desires the vineyard of Naboth, a foreigner living next to him. Ahab offers to buy the land or trade for it but Naboth refuses. Ahab's idolatrous wife Jezebel then schemes to have Naboth falsely accused and stoned to death. In this way, Ahab gains possession of Naboth's vineyard but God curses him through the prophet Elijah:

> Then the word of the LORD came to Elijah the Tishbite: "Go down to meet Ahab king of Israel, who rules in Samaria. He is now in Naboth's vineyard, where he has gone to take possession of it. Say to him, 'This is what the LORD says: Have you not murdered a man and seized his property?' Then say to him, 'This is what the LORD says: In the place where dogs licked up Naboth's blood, dogs will lick up your blood—yes, yours!'[30]

Ateek draws a connection between the actions of the wicked King Ahab and the actions of the modern State of Israel:

> Theologically speaking, the State of Israel has been guilty of the same misdeed as Ahab... Yahweh's ethical law, championed by the Prophets, operated impartially: every person's rights, property, and very life were under divine protection. Whenever injustice occurred, God intervened to defend the poor, the weak, and the defenseless.[31]

Ateek calls on the Christian Church to condemn injustices committed against Palestinians and to promote peace and justice within Israel-Palestine. Palestinian Christians are called to non-violent resistance. The same year that Ateek published *Justice, and Only Justice*, he founded the Sabeel Ecumenical Liberation Theology Center in Jerusalem which seeks to promote Palestinian Liberation Theology through advocacy, conferences, and education. The Center also publically opposed the Iraq War. Sabeel has a wide network of supporters including a "Friends of Sabeel" chapter in the United States.

Although Ateek is not a U.S. citizen and does not serve with an American missionary organization, his writings and efforts are an example of how American missionary activity can inadvertently have political consequences. Ateek was educated at schools founded by Southern Baptists and Presbyterians and he is a leader within the Palestinian Protestant community—a community created through missionary efforts. [32] His theological arguments against Zionism draw on beliefs and techniques common to American Protestants and his efforts have been supported by some within the American missionary community. World Vision's former director in Jerusalem, Tom Gettman, serves on the steering committee for the American Friends of Sabeel chapter. Jonathan Kuttub, the Chairman of the Board for the Bethlehem Bible College, is a U.S. citizen and member of Sabeel's executive committee. Ateek also spoke at the first *Christ at the Checkpoint Conference.*

Impact of International Politics on Mission Work

One of key intersections between politics and mission work in Israel/Palestine is travel visas and government permits. The State of Israel legally permits missionary work but, at the same time, strongly discourages it. Many of those interviewed said Israeli government officials attempt to hinder mission work by denying visas and travel permits under false pretenses. Enforcement of policies is also reportedly inconsistent and the U.S. Department of State's International Religious Freedom Report describes the situation as follows:

> Proselytizing is legal in the country and missionaries of all religious groups are allowed to proselytize all citizens; however, a 1977 law prohibits any person from offering

material benefits as an inducement to conversion. It was also illegal to convert persons under 18 years of age unless one parent were an adherent of the religious group seeking to convert the minor. Despite the legality of proselytism, the government has taken a number of steps that encouraged the perception that proselytizing is against government policy. For example, the Ministry of the Interior (MOI) has detained individuals suspected of being "missionaries," and required of such persons bail and a pledge to abstain from missionary activity, in addition to refusing them entry into the country... The MOI has also cited proselytism as a reason to deny student, work, and religious visa extensions, as well as to deny permanent residency petitions.[33]

Because the Ministry of the Interior (MOI) has authority over population issues including citizenship, immigration and visas, Israeli political parties with strong religious views fight for control of it. Many interviewees reported than when an ultra-orthodox party controls the MOI, it is much harder for missionaries to obtain visas and permits.

In Palestine, the Palestinian Authority (PA) opposes missionary efforts but the legal environment is vague. Palestinian Basic Law, the temporary constitution of Palestine, holds that Islam is the official religion and that Islamic Sharia is to be the principle source of all legislation.[34] (Hamas has gone so far as to declare Sharia law to be in effect but with mixed enforcement.) Other religions are to be "respected." In any event, the PA has relatively little authority and interviewees did not report that it interfered with mission efforts.

Government recognition of religions is another way politics influences mission work. Israeli law traces its roots back to the Ottoman "Millet System" which established separate, autonomous jurisdictions for each confessional community. The British mandate maintained the system until 1948 and modern Israeli law has separate Religious Courts for each recognized religious denomination. The Religious Courts have jurisdiction over "personal status" matters such as marriage, divorce, guardianship and adoption. Recognized religions also enjoy tax benefits, budget allocations within the Ministry of Religious Affairs, more autonomy in church governance, greater access to public officials, and official recognition of converts.

The Anglican Church is the only recognized Protestant denomination in Israel and, as a result, most of the religious communities built by American missionaries have a disadvantageous legal standing.[35] Several interviewees cited marriage as one area particularly affected by the distinction. Without official recognition, non-Anglican Protestants wanting to marry must go through additional bureaucratic procedures. The U.S. Embassy in Israel describes the conditions as follows:

> Only the religious communities mentioned above have de jure status in Israel. Other groups, including Protestant churches, have only de facto recognition; and in the absence of specific legislation on the subject, marriage between Protestants is arranged on ad hoc and individual basis.
>
> The minister who plans to perform the ceremony writes to the Ministry for Religious Affairs, setting forth the names

of the persons to be married, their nationality, and their religious affiliation. He requests the Ministry's permission to perform the marriage and to issue a marriage certificate. Protestants planning to be married in Israel should allow from two to four weeks to complete the formalities required before the marriage can take place.[36]

School curriculums are another area where Protestant converts are at a disadvantage. In 2006, the Israeli government formulated a new Christian curriculum for students in public and private high schools. Evangelical groups objected to it and claimed its teachings conflicted with their theology. Moreover, instructors could only be drawn from recognized religious communities—a provision that prevented evangelicals from presenting their own doctrines in evangelical schools.[37] Despite the objections, the curriculum was unmodified. The Evangelical Council of Israel which includes the Baptist, Assembly of God, Brethren, and Church of the Nazarene denominations is lobbying for official recognition of an evangelical denomination in Israeli.

U.S. foreign policy and the Arab-Israeli conflict also have a considerable and multifaceted impact on American mission work. Palestinians (and Arabs in general) associate Protestant Christianity with America and U.S. political support for Israel. This casts it in a negative light because most Palestinians vehemently feel U.S. policy is unfair and biased against them. As a result, missionaries must delicately discuss the subject of politics when speaking to Palestinians. Most interviewees said the topic should be assiduously avoided.

In similar fashion, pastors and missionaries must carefully discuss Old Testament passages, given their association with Christian Zionism and U.S. political support for Israel. Dispensationalism is a "dirty word" and some Palestinians believe that Christianity teaches God loves Jews more than Arabs. One interviewee said that he was asked not to discuss the Old Testament at all while guest-preaching at an Arab church.[38]

The association between Protestant Christianity and U.S. foreign policy casts suspicion on Palestinian Protestants. One interviewee said Palestinian Protestants must continually apologize for and condemn anti-Islamic statements made by Americans—the recent burning of a Koran by a Florida pastor was cited as an example.[39] In similar fashion, Palestinian Protestants vocalize support for a Palestinian state in order to alleviate doubts.[40]

Political factors complicate the social and religious tensions between Muslims and Christians seeking to convert Muslims. These tensions are, on rare occasions, punctuated by acts of violence. In 2007, for example, Rami Ayyad—an Arab Protestant—was abducted and killed by Muslim extremists. Ayyad ran the only Christian bookshop in the Gaza Strip on behalf of the Protestant Holy Bible Society—a Christian mission organization.[41] In response, many leaders of the Baptist church he attended fled to Jordan.[42] At the same time, the act was condemned by both Palestinian Christians and Muslims. A spokesman for Hamas' Interior Ministry called it a "despicable crime" and warned the perpetrators would be "severely punished."[43] Mahmoud Abbas, the President of the Palestinian National Authority, condemned the attack as "barbaric" and blamed it on Hamas' militia forces.[44]

Despite the negative connotations Protestant Christianity acquires from U.S. foreign policy, none of the interviewees believe U.S. policy is a major obstacle to winning converts or building strong relationships with Palestinians. Most said Palestinians draw a distinction between the American government and individual Americans. Political preconceptions dissipate once individual relationships are formed. The process is slow but not unduly difficult. Interviewees also generally reported that no matter what preconceptions are held, Palestinians treat Americans cordially from the beginning—a characteristic attributed to the strong cultural emphasis on hospitality.

Politics not only creates tensions with Palestinian Muslims but also within the Christian community. Arab Protestants generally support an independent Palestinian state; Messianic Jews usually support Israeli settlers and conservative policies.[45] Political differences thus sharply divide the tiny Protestant minority in Israel/Palestine and make it difficult for the two groups to cooperate even on issues in which they have common interests.

Some efforts have been made to bring the two sides together. Masalaha, an organization operated by Messianic Jews and Palestinian Protestants, aims to build closer ties between the two communities. It organizes a variety of camps and events which bring people from both sides together to study Biblical principles of reconciliation and to discuss differences. Of note, Salim Munayer, the organization's founder, is a faculty member of the Bethlehem Bible College.

Politics creates tensions between American missionaries and churches. Missionaries working with Palestinians are generally critical of Israeli policies and Christian Zionism in particular. Most lament that Christian Zionism "unconditionally" supports Israel. "Blind approval of Israel is not good," commented one.[46] Another exclaimed, "I don't blindly support my *own* government."[47] Many emphasized Israel's secular culture as a reason to limit political support. "They are not a God fearing or God honoring country."[48] Others completely rejected Christian Zionism. One called it a "heresy" and pointed out that the Biblical prophets sharply criticized ancient Israel for acting unjustly.[49] Another said that Jesus himself sharply criticized Jewish political authorities. The connection between Biblical Jews and the modern state of Israel was "vague" in the opinion of one. Christian Zionism was "really radical" and "I can't go along at all" with it.[50] Most interviewees believe that Palestinians are unjustly treated by the Israeli government and army. They also contend that the United States government is overly supporting of Israel.

Missionary criticisms of Israel and Christian Zionism appear directly tied to their experiences in the region. Some interviewees said their mission experiences had substantially changed their personal political views and they are now more sympathetic to the Palestinian perspective. Several others who had lived in the region prior to engaging in mission work note that American missionaries usually become more sympathetic to the Palestinian perspective after experiencing their living conditions.

Political views create internal divisions within the mission's movement. Several interviewees report that there are tensions between those working among Palestinians and those working among Jews because of the sharply contrasting political views held by each—those working among Palestinians are more pro-Arab, those working among Jews are more pro-Israel. Political divisions also create tensions between the missionaries and the American churches that financially support their efforts. Guth notes that American Evangelicals are generally supportive of Israel.[51] Missionary criticisms of Israel and Christian Zionism thus stand in sharp contrast with the movement's base. The tensions caused by this political gap manifest in several ways. For example, several interviewees are uncomfortable expressing their political and theological views to domestic supporters. Premillennial dispensationalism was a particularly sensitive topic because of its implications for the State of Israel. Other interviewees are more open about their views but they occasionally receive harsh criticisms in response. Several report occasions when they were speaking before church groups and were interrupted and accosted by angry parishioners. One (from a main-line denomination) said he dreaded discussing his mission experiences before church groups because he was so often criticized. This case aside, most interviewees said they receive a welcome response from church groups more often than not. Only one interviewee said he had actually lost financial support because of his political views.[52]

Summary

Politics directly influences American mission work to Palestinians through the visa process. When religious political parties control the Israeli Ministry of Interior, it is harder for missionaries to obtain permits and visas. Many Palestinian Protestants, such as the Baptists and the Assemblies of God, are also not granted full equality under Israeli law because they are not part of an officially recognized religious denomination.

Politics also indirectly influences American mission work by creating internal divisions within the movement. There are strong tensions between Jewish and Arab Protestants because of the Mid-East conflict; tensions between the American missionaries that work with Jews and those that work with Palestinians; and tensions between the missionaries and their domestic supporters. In similar fashion, Palestinian Protestants are often treated with suspicion by Palestinian Muslims because of American political support for Israel.

American mission work to Palestinians has a minor influence on politics. The missionary ranks provide a small pool of advocates for the Palestinian people. Thus far, their efforts have yielded little political fruit but it is fostering a small but growing movement among American Evangelicals to have a more balanced foreign policy towards Israel.

American mission work also has some political influence through the institutions that spring from it. Palestinian Protestants, with support from American churches and missionaries, have established many entities that serve as hubs of Palestinian advocacy including, most notably, the Bethlehem Bible College. This development is strikingly similar to events that occurred during the turn of the century when missionary schools became centers of Arab nationalism—a movement that ultimately had a substantial political impact. This limited political influence of contemporary institutions may grow if history is any indicator of the future. Having analyzed both historical mission work in the Middle East and three case studies on contemporary work, I will now present my conclusions on the relationship between mission work and international politics and how those conclusions contribute to scholarship on religion and international politics.

---

[1] A.L. Tibawi, *American Interests in Syria, 1800-1901* (Oxford: Clarendon Press, 1966), 105.

[2] Paul M. Blowers, "Living in a Land of Prophets: James T. Barclay and an Early Disciples of Christ Mission to the Jews in the Holy Land," *Church History 62*, no. 4 (Dec 1993): 497, 503.

[3] Roy H. Kreider, *Land of Revelation* (Scottdale: Herald Press, 2004), 69; Eric N. Newberg, "The Palestine Missionary Band and the Azusa-Jerusalem Connection," *Journal of the European Pentecostal Theological Association 2011*, no 1.

[4] Southern Baptist Convention, *Resolution on Evangelism*, (May 1896). http://www.sbc.net/resolutions/amResolution.asp?ID=500 (accessed February 13, 2012).

[5] Mussa had been raised in Eastern Christian tradition.

[6] David Smith, "Baptist in the Holy Land," *The Jerusalem Post* (March 9, 2007).

[7] Lanier Theological Library, "Robert Lindset Collection," http://www.laniertheologicallibrary.org/robert_lindsey/ (accessed November 26, 2011).

[8] Kreider, *Land of Revelation*, 43, 83.

[9] During the 1990s, the Southern Baptist mission board and the local Baptists churches wrangled over the ownership of the facility and the price at which the former would sell to the latter. In the end, through a generous personal donation of Dwight Baker, a longtime Baptist missionary to Israel, the home was acquired by the local Baptist churches and converted into a seminary.

[10] Christians of any sort comprise 1.6% of the population; Mandryk, Operation World, 665.

[11] Alain Epp Weaver, ed. *Under Vine and Fig Tree: Biblical Theologies of Land and the Palestinian-Israeli Conflict*, (Telford: Cascadia Publishing House, 2007), 145.

[12] Andrew Bush, "The Implications of Christian Zionism for Mission, " *International Bulletin of Missionary Research*, 33.3 (July 2009): 149.

[13] Tom Gettman, "Heeding the Bethlehem Call: Freedom Comes from Tenacity," *God's Politics: A blog by Jim Wallis and Friends*, (December 23, 2011). http://sojo.net/blogs/2011/12/23/heeding-bethlehem-call-freedom-comes-tenacity (accessed March 3, 2012).

[14] Bob Stanley, "Parks Takes Strong Stand Against Israel Resolution," *Baptist Press*, (February 9, 1983).

[15] Ibid.

[16] Jerilynn Armstrong, "Stanley, Draper, Smith Repudiate Farrakhan," *Baptist Press*, (July 5, 1984).

[17] Ibid.

[18] NorthWood Church Glocal.net, "Foot Washing Interview with Bishara Awad," (February 11, 2008). http://www.glocal.net/blog/comments/foot-washing-interview-with-bishara-awad/ (accessed February 13, 2012).

[19] Christ at the Checkpoint, "Bishara Awad," http://www.christatthecheckpoint.com/index.php/ speakers/59-bishara-awad (accessed February 13, 2012).

[20] Global Ministries: The United Methodist Church, "Alex Awad." http://new.gbgm-umc.org/work/missionaries/biographies/index.cfm?id=26 (accessed February 13, 2012).

[21] "Labib Madanat Joins American Bible Society," *Record Online: Digital Magazine of the American Bible Society.* http://record.americanbible.org/content/around-world/labib-madanat-joins-american-bible-society (accessed February 13, 2012).

[22] Holy Land Trust, "About Us." http://www.holylandtrust.org/index.php?option=com_content&task=view&id=191&Itemid=144 (accessed February 13, 2012).

[23] Jonathan Kuttab, "Steps to create an Israel-Palestine," *Los Angeles Times,* (December 20, 2009). http://articles.latimes.com/2009/dec/20/opinion/la-oe-kuttab20-2009dec20 (accessed February 13, 2012).

[24] Jonathan Kuttub, "Arab Christians are nationalists, not 'fifth-columnists'," *The Daily Star,* (November 28, 2005). http://www.dailystar.com.lb/Opinion/Commentary/Nov/28/Arab-Christians-are-nationalists-not-fifth-columnists.ashx#axzz1leMERxS9 (accessed February 13, 2012).

[25] Alex Awad, "Why Christians Need to Support Palestinian Drive Towards Statehood." http://www.alexawad.org/details.php?ID=26 (accessed February 13, 2012).

[26] Christ at the Checkpoint, "Conference Goals." http://www.christatthecheckpoint.com/ index.php/about-us/conference-goals (accessed February 13, 2012).

[27] Naim Stifan Ateek, *Justice and only Justice,* (Maryknoll, Orbis Books, 1989), 8.

[28] Ateek, *Justice and only Justice,* 9-12.

[29] Ibid., 88.

[30] 1 Kings 21:17-19.

[31] Ateek, *Justice and only Justice,* 88.

[32] Nazareth Baptist School and Hardin-Simmons are both Baptist institutions. The San Francisco Theological Seminary was established by Presbyterians (PC USA).

[33] U.S. Department of State, *International Religious Freedom Report 2010: Israel and the Occupied Territories*, November 17, 2010. http://www.state.gov/g/drl/rls/irf/2010/148825.htm (accessed February 13, 2012).

[34] "The Palestinian Basic Law is to function as a temporary constitution for the Palestinian Authority until the establishment of an independent state and a permanent constitution for Palestine can be achieved. The Basic Law was passed by the Palestinian Legislative Council in 1997 and ratified by President Yasser Arafat in 2002."; Erik Bolstad and Tonje M. Vikren, "The Palestinian Basic Law." http:// www.palestinianbasiclaw.org/ (accessed April 4, 2012).

[35] Shimon Shetreet, "Freedom of Religion in Israel." http://www.mfa.gov.il/MFA/MFAArchive/ 2000_2009/2001/8/Freedom%20of%20Religion%20in%20Israel (accessed October 13, 2012).

[36] Embassy of the United States: Tel Aviv Israel, *Marriage in Israel.* http://israel.usembassy.gov/ consular/acs/marriage.html (accessed February 13, 2012).

[37] Sheryl Henderson Blunt, "Marginalized Again," *Christianity Today* (November 17, 2006). http://www.christianitytoday.com/ct/2006/december/1.15.html (accessed February 13, 2012).

[38] Telephone interview with individual involved in mission work in the Middle East, Dallas, TX, January 19, 2012.

[39] In March of 2011, the pastor of a small church put the Koran on "trial" and burned it after he found it to be "guilty."

[40] Telephone interview with individual involved in mission work in the Middle East, Dallas, January 12, 2012.

[41] "Christian activist slain in Hamas controlled Gaza," Israel Ministry of Foreign Affairs (October 8, 2007). http://www.mfa.gov.il/MFA/Terrorism-+Obstacle+to+Peace/Terror+Groups/Christian+activist +slain+in+Hamas+controlled+Gaza+8-Oct-2007.htm (accessed November 26, 2011).

[42] Telephone interview with individual involved in mission work in the Middle East, Dallas, TX, November 8, 2011.

[43] Khaled Abu Toameh, "Christian Official Found Slain in Gaza," *The Jerusalem Post,* (October 8, 2007).

[44] Israel Ministry of Foreign Affairs, "Christian Activist Slain in Hamas Controlled Gaza," (October 8, 2007). http://www.mfa.gov.il/MFA/Terrorism-+Obstacle+to+Peace/Terror+Groups/Christian+

activist+slain+in+Hamas+controlled+Gaza+8-Oct-2007.htm (accessed February 13, 2012).

[45] Messianic Jews adhere to Jewish religious traditions but otherwise hold theological doctrines common to evangelical Protestants including the divine inspiration of the New Testament; Messianic Jewish Alliance of America, "Statement of Faith." http://www.mjaa.org/site/PageServer?pagename=n_about_us_statement_of_faith (accessed August 4, 2012).

[46] Telephone interview with individual involved in mission work in the Middle East, Dallas TX, October 15, 2011.

[47] Telephone interview with individual raised in a missionary family in the Middle East, Dallas TX, November 16, 2011.

[48] Telephone interview with individual involved in mission work in the Middle East, Dallas, TX, October 15, 2011.

[49] Interview with individual involved in mission work in the Middle East, Ft. Worth, TX, November 2, 2011.

[50] Interview with individual involved in mission work in the Middle East, Dallas, TX, November 16, 2011.

[51] James L. Guth, "Religious Religious Leadership and Support for Israel: A Study of Clergy in Nineteen Denominations," paper, Southern Political Science Association, New Orleans, January 3-7, 2007).

[52] Telephone interview with individual involved in mission work in the Middle East, Dallas, TX, January 17, 2012.

Chapter 6: Conclusions

The relationship between politics and American mission work in the Middle East is lopsided and at times almost unidirectional. That is to say, politics has a tremendous impact on American mission work; American mission work usually has minimal impact on politics. At one level, the influence of political factors is unsurprising. Wars, revolutions, and government policies on visas and human rights open and close the door to American mission work. World War I and its succeeding events wiped out a century of American mission work in Eastern Turkey and Northern Iran. The Gulf War and Iraq War, conversely, opened the door to work by establishing an American military presence in Iraq. The political ascent of Kemal Ataturk and Reza Shah severely limited American mission work in Turkey and Iran, respectively. The 1979 Iranian revolution eliminated the American presence in Iran altogether. The political ascent of Orthodox Jewish parties in Israel hinders the missionaries' ability to obtain visas. The relationship between politics and mission work at this level is straightforward. Conflict prevents or destroys mission work in the short run. The presence of Western military powers (be they British or American) has on several occasions opened the door to mission work by safeguarding mission organizations. Regional governments set the terms on which American NGOs, including mission organizations, are permitted to operate in the country.

Politics can also have a divisive effect on the missionary movement by separating erstwhile allies. Missionaries working among the Palestinians report tensions between themselves and their domestic supporters in the U.S. because of political differences. American missionaries working among the Palestinians are sympathetic to the Palestinian perspective of the Arab-Israeli conflict. American Protestant churches, on the other hand, are sympathetic to the Israeli perspective. In similar fashion, Palestinian Protestants and Israeli Protestants do not cooperate with each others because of their sharp political differences.

At another level, politics influences American mission work in ways that are profound, under-recognized, and arguably more lasting. World War I brought the first wave of American mission work to an end by shattering its religious and theological foundation. The sight of "Christian" nations engaged in war, and with the vigorous support of the American church, triggered a "religious depression" that threw the missionary enterprise into reverse. Long-established mission organizations like the ABCFM and BFMPC withered; the once-mighty SVM died. In the same vein, oppression at the hands of Muslims (even nominal ones like Saddam Hussein) reportedly breathes life into American mission efforts by making the mission field ripe for the harvest. Missionaries generally claim that Saddam Hussein's oppression of the Kurds of Northern Iraq fostered disillusionment with Islam and a degree of openness to Christianity. Statistically, these claims cannot be verified but it is notable that Northern Iraq is home to one of the few, legally recognized, Protestant Churches in the world that is comprised of converted Muslims. Likewise in Iran, interviewees consistently report that the government's brutal efforts to Islamize society have led to a significant number of Muslims converting to Protestant Christianity. These claims, once again, cannot be empirically verified given the paucity of data, but is it notable that academic and government works have documented cases of conversion within Iran.

The significance of these events, should they ultimately prove true, would be substantial. American Protestants have attempted to convert Muslims since they first arrived in the region nearly two hundred years ago. They had limited success in establishing self-sustaining congregations of Orthodox and Catholic Christian converts but they failed to established self-sustaining congregations of Muslims converts. Today they appear to be realizing that goal.

The collapse of the missions movement after World War I, the reported receptiveness of Kurd's to Christianity following Saddam Hussein's oppression and the reported receptiveness of Iranians to Christianity following the Iranian Revolution, suggest that major political events can dramatically impact mission efforts by fostering negative perceptions about a religion. Warfare between Christians in World War I greatly disillusioned American Christians and undermined the missions movement. Political oppression is allegedly disillusioning Kurdish and Iranian Muslims and encouraging them to consider Christianity. Political events, in other words, may have alternatively led to the American missionary enterprise's greatest reversals and its greatest successes.[1]

The influence of American mission work on politics is usually minimal. Missionaries have a poor track record of lobbying policy makers. They reached the pinnacle of their influence during the Wilson presidency and even then failed to achieve most of their goals. Missionary efforts to provide self-determination for Arabs and Armenians failed. Calls for American mandates in the Middle East went unheeded. Efforts to ratify the Treaty of Sevres failed. Following World War II, their influence declined when other issues rose to prominence. The Cold War, the Arab-Israeli conflict, terrorism and oil became the U.S. government's top political concerns in the region. American mission work no longer constituted a significant political interest.

American missionaries in the region have achieved only a few major political victories. Based on their vigorous counsel and vocal opposition to war with Turkey, the U.S. government did not declare war on Turkey during World War I. Likewise following the war, the missionaries were briefly able to secure provisions for an independent Armenia. The victory proved pyrrhic, however, and such a state never emerged. The missionaries did have access to the Ottoman Empire thanks to political pressure exerted on their behalf by the U.S. and British governments. And yet political pressure was never enough to allow the evangelization of Muslims and was eventually off-set by a more assertive Kemalist government.

Added to the larger successes are a few minor political victories. Missionaries have been able to help their overseas parishioners obtain visas to immigrate to the U.S.—most notably in the case of operation Pacific Haven which evacuated Kurds from Northern Iraq. They have also advocated on behalf of persecuted Christians in the Middle East (sometimes quietly, sometimes publically) with some success.

While missionary lobbying efforts are typically unsuccessful, mission work has had a larger political influence through the schools it creates. The American University in Cairo and the American University in Beirut became centers of Arab nationalism. Bosphorus University became a center of Bulgarian nationalism and Turkish nationalism. These movements eventually reshaped the political landscape of the Middle East and they underscore several salient points about the political influence of mission work.

These movements illustrate how the greatest political impact of American mission work is not through its evangelistic

efforts but rather through its educational efforts. The local
population, for the most part, rejected the religious message of
the missionaries. At the same time, Western conceptions of
science, government, and economics took root and gave birth to
the nationalistic movements that sprang from the mission
schools.

These movements illustrate how the political impact of
mission work is not immediate but long-term in nature. The
missions movement began emphasizing educational efforts
around 1870 after Rufus Anderson, a longtime proponent of
"Christianizing," left the ABCFM. With his departure, the
emphasis shifted to "civilizing" mission fields and the number of
schools quickly multiplied. Nevertheless, it took years for the
political effects of the shift to be felt. The Young Turk rebellion
and Bulgarian independence occurred in 1908, nearly forty years
later. The Arab Revolt occurred even later in 1916 and Arab
nationalist governments did not come to power until after World
War II.

These movements also illustrate that the primary political
impact of mission work is enabling local political activism.
Mission schools drew together and politicized a constituency that
eventually gained power in many nations. The constituencies
were strongly influenced by Western ideas and yet still held
domestic expressions of political will. The missionaries,
moreover, politically supported these constituencies even in cases
when the American Protestant Church held contrary views:

missionaries publically opposed Zionism at a time when the domestic church was publically supporting it.

The political impact of first wave mission work raises questions about the political impact of second wave mission work. The second wave of mission effort has had scant political impact thus far, but its educational efforts bear resemblance to the first wave efforts that eventually had a larger influence. For example, the Bethlehem Bible College has become a center of political activism with missionaries and Western church leaders supporting its Palestinian perspective of the Mid-East conflict. Servant Group International is establishing a chain of schools in Northern Iraq that could one day become similar centers of political activity. It is still too early to see if the schools founded by second-wave missionaries will have a similar impact as the schools founded by their first-wave forbears.

To conclude, there is a strong relationship between international politics and American mission work in the Middle East, but the relationship is misunderstood. Politics has a substantial short-term impact on mission work by shaping where and how it can be conducted. It also can have a profound long-term impact on mission work by influencing perceptions of Christianity and Islam. Mission work, for its part, has little short term political impact. Missionaries do not carry decisive political weight and their evangelistic message is simply dismissed by most of the local population. At the same time, it can have lasting long-term impact, but that impact stems from its educational efforts (which enable political activism) rather than its evangelistic efforts.

---

[1] This finding is consistent with the view offered by James Barton, the influential head of the ABCFM. He argued (as discussed in chapter 3) that Western, political machinations fostered a negative perception of Christianity in the Middle East and were the reason Muslims were not converting to Christianity.

Bibliography

Books

Abrams, Elliot, ed. *The Influence of Faith: Religious Groups and U.S. Foreign Policy* . Lanham: Rowman & Littlefield Publishers, 2001.

Albright, Madeline. *The Mighty and the Almighty: Reflections of America, God, and World Affairs.* New York: Harper Perennial, 2007.

Almond, Gabriel A. & R. Scott Appleby. *Strong Religion: The Rise of Fundamentalisms around the World.* Chicago: University of Chicago Press, 2003.

Anderson, Gerald H. *Biographical Dictionary of Christian Missions.* Grand Rapids: William B. Eerdmans Publishing Company, 1998.

Anderson, Rufus. *Foreign Missions: Their Relations and Claims.* New York: Charles Scribner and Company, 1869.

Anderson, Rufus. *History of the Missions of the American Board of Commissioners for Foreign Missions to the Oriental Churches*, Vol. 1. Boston: Congregational Publishing Society, 1872.

Ateek, Naim Stifan *Justice and only Justice.* Maryknoll: Orbis Books, 1989.

Barber, Benjamin. *Jihad vs. McWorld: How Globalism and Tribalism Are Reshaping the World.* New York: Ballantine Books, 1996.

Barclay, J.T. *The City of the Great King: Jerusalem As It Was, As It Is, and As It Is to Be.* Philadelphia: James Challen and Sons. 1858.

Barton, James L. *The Christian Approach to Islam.* Boston: The Pilgrim Press, 1918.

———. *Daybreak in Turkey.* Boston: The Pilgrim Press, 1908.

Berger, Peter L., ed. *The Desecularization of the World: Resurgent Religion and World Politics.* Washington, D.C.: Ethics and Public Policy Center, 1999.

———. *The Sacred Canopy: Elements of a Sociological Theory of Religion.* Doubleday: Anchor Books, 1967.

Berger, Peter L. & Samuel P. Huntington, ed. *Many Globalizations: Cultural Diversity in the Contemporary World.* New York: Oxford University Press, 2002.

Blincoe, Robert. *Ethnic Realities and the Church: Lessons from Kurdistan.* Pasadena: Presbyterian Center for Mission Studies. 1998.

Bosch, David Jacobus. *Transforming Mission: Paradigm Shifts in Theology of Mission.* Maryknoll: Orbis Books, 1991.

Brackney, William H. *Baptist in North America: A Historical Perspective.* Malden: Blackwell Publishing, 2006.

Brother Andrew and Al Janssen. *Light Force: A Stirring Account of the Church Caught in the Middle East Crossfire.* Grand Rapids: Fleming H. Revell, 2004.

Brouwer, Steve, Paul Gifford, & Susan D. Rose. *Exporting the American Gospel: Global Christian Fundamentalism.* New York: Routledge, 1996.

The Commission of Appraisal. *Re-Thinking Missions: A Laymen's Inquiry After One Hundred Years.* New York: Harper & Brothers Publishers, 1932.

Danish Refugee Council. *Human Rights Situation for Minorities, Women and Converts, end Entry and Exit Procedures, ID Cards, Summons and Reporting, etc. Fact finding mission to*

Iran 24th August – 2nd September 2008. Copenhagen: April 2009.

Dark, K.R., ed. *Religion and International Relations.* New York: Palgrace, 2000.

DeNovo, John. *American Interests and Policies in the Middle East: 1900-1939.* Minneapolis: The University of Minnesota Press, 1963.

Dione, E.J., Jean Bethke Elshtain and Kayla Drogosz, ed. *Liberty and Power: A Dialogue on Religion and U.S. Foreign Policy in an Unjust World.* Washington: Brookings Institution Press, 2004.

Doğan, Mehmet Ali and Heather J. Sharkey, ed. *American Missionaries and the Middle East: Foundational Encounters.* Salt Lake City: The University of Utah Press, 2011.

Doyle, Tom. *Breakthrough: The Return of Hope to the Middle East.* Colorado Springs: Authentic, 2008.

Dwight, H. G. O. *Christianity in Turkey a Narrative of the Protestant Reformation in the Armenian Church.* London: James Nisbet & Co., 1854.

Elder, John. *History of the Iran Mission.* New York: Literature Committee of the Church Council of Iran, 1960.

Farr, Thomas. *World of Faith and Freedom: Why International Religious Liberty Is Vital to American National Security.* New York: Oxford University Press, 2008.

Gamble, Richard M. *The War for Righteousness: Progressive Christianity, the Great War, and the Rise of the Messianic Nation.* Wilmington: ISI Books, 2003.

Grabill, Joseph L. *Protestant Diplomacy and the Near East: Missionary Influence on American Policy, 1810-1927.* Minneapolis: University of Minnesota Press, 1971.

Hertzke, Allen D. *Freeing God's Children: The Unlikely Alliance for Global Human Rights.* Lanham: Rowman & Littlefield Publishers, Inc. 2006.

Huntington, Samuel P. *The Clash of Civilizations and the Remaking of World Order*. New York: Touchstone, 1997.

Hutchison, William R. *Errand to the World: American Protestant Thought and Foreign Missions*. Chicago: University of Chicago Press, 1987.

Hurst, Dick. *Religion, An Accident of Birth*. Bloomington: Jones Harvest Publishing, 2008.

Inboden, William III. *Religion and American Foreign Policy, 1945-1960: The Soul of Containment*. New York: Cambridge University Press, 2008.

Jewett, Robert. *Mission and Menace: Four Centuries of American Religious Zeal*. Minneapolis: Fortress Press, 2008.

Juergensmeyer, Mark. *The New Cold War? Religious Nationalism Confronts the Secular State*. Berkley: University of California Press, 1994.

———. *Terror in the Mind of God: The Global Rise of Religious Violence*. Berkeley: University of California Press, 2003.

Kaplan, Robert. *The Arabists*. New York: The Free Press, 1993.

Kepel, Giles. *The Revenge of God: The Resurgence of Islam, Christianity and Judaism in the Modern World*, Cambridge: Polity Press, 1994.

Kieser, Hans-Lukas. *Nearest East: American Millennialism and Mission to the Middle East*. Philadelphia: Temple University Press, 2010.

"King-Crane report on the Near East." In *Editor & publisher*. New York: Editor & Publisher Co., 1922.

Kreider, Roy H. *Land of Revelation A Reconciling Presence in Israel*. Scottdale: Herald Press, 2004.

Lewis, Bernard. *What Went Wrong?: The Clash Between Islam and Modernity in the Middle East*. New York: Harper Perennial, 2002.

Magee, Malcom. *What the World Should Be: Woodrow Wilson and the Crafting of Faith-based Foreign Policy.* Waco: Baylor University Press, 2008.

Makdisi, Ussama. *Artillery of Heaven: American Missionaries and the Failed Conversion of the Middle East.* New York: Cornell University Press, 2008.

————. *Faith Misplaced: The Broken Promise of U.S.-Arab Relations, 1820-2001.* New York: Public Affairs, 2010.

Marsden, Lee. *For God's Sake: The Christian Right and the US Foreign Policy.* London: Zed Books, 2008.

Marty, Martin E. and R. Scott Appleby, ed. *Accounting for Fundamentalisms: The Dynamic Character of Movements.* Chicago: The University of Chicago Press, 2004.

Marty, Martin E. and R. Scott Appleby, ed. *Fundamentalisms and Society: Reclaiming the Sciences, the Family, and Education.* Chicago: The University of Chicago Press, 1993.

Marty, Martin E. and R. Scott Appleby, ed. *Fundamentalisms and the State: Remaking Polities, Economies, and Militance.* Chicago: The University of Chicago Press, 1996.

Mansoori, Ahmad. "American Missionaries in Iran, 1834-1934." Ph.D. diss., Ball State University, 1986.

Marty, Martin E. and R. Scott Appleby, ed. *Fundamentalisms Comprehended.* Chicago: The University of Chicago Press, 1995.

Marty, Martin E. and R. Scott Appleby, ed. *Fundamentalisms Observed.* Chicago: The University of Chicago Press, 1994.

Merkley, Paul Charles. *The Politics of Christian Zionism, 1891-1948.* London: Frank Cass Publishers, 1998.

Michlewait, John & Wooldridge, Adrian. *God is Back.* New York: The Penguin Press, 2009.

Mullican, Kenneth R., Jr. and Loren C. Turnage. *One Foot in Heaven: The Story of Bob Lindsey of Jerusalem.* Baltimore: Publish America, 2005.

Murphy, Lawrence R. *The American University in Cairo, 1919-1987.* Cairo: The American University in Cairo Press, 1987.

Murre–van den Berg, Heleen, ed. *New Faith in Ancient Lands: Western Missions in the Middle East in the Nineteenth and Early Twentieth Centuries.* Leiden: Brill, 2006.

Nichols, J. Bruce. *The Uneasy Alliance: Religion, Refugee Work, and U.S. Foreign Policy.* New York: Oxford University Press, 1988.

Norway, Country of Origin Information Center (Landinfo). *Report Iran: Christians and Converts.* Oslo, July 7, 2011.

Oren, Michael B. *Power, Faith, and Fantasy: America in the Middle East, 1776 to the Present Day.* New York: Norton & Company, 2007.

Patterson, James Allan. "Robert E. Speer and the Crisis of the American Protestant Missionary Movement, 1920-1937." Ph.D. diss., Princeton Theological Seminary, 1980.

Pikkert, Pieter. "Protestant Missionaries to the Middle East: Ambassadors of Christ or Culture?" Ph.D. diss., University of South Africa, 2006.

Pullen, Larry L. *Christian Ethics and U.S. Foreign Policy: The Helsinki Accords and Human Rights.* Lanham: Lexington Books, 2000.

Register, Ray G. *Back to Jerusalem: Church Planting Movements in the Holy Land.* Enumclaw: WinePress, 2000.

Richards, Thomas Cole. *The Haystack Prayer Meeting: An Account of its Origin and Spirit.* Boston: The Haystack Centennial Committee, 1906.

Roy, Olivier. *Globalized Islam: The Search for a New Ummah.* New York: Columbia University Press, 2004.

Safa, Reza. *The Coming Fall of Islam in Iran,* Lake Mary: FrontLine, 2006.

Showalter, Nathan D. *The End of a Crusade: The Student Volunteer Movement for Foreign Missions and the Great War*. Lanham: Scarecrow Press. 1997.

Spellman, Kathryn. *Religion and Nation: Iranian Local and Transnational Networks in Britain*. New York: Bergham Books, 2004.

Taylor, Gordon. *Fever & Thirst: A Missionary Doctor Among the Tribes of Kurdistan*. Chicago: Academy Chicago Publishers, 2005.

Thomas, Scott M. *The Global Resurgence of Religion and the Transformation of International Relations: The Struggle for the Soul of the Twenty-First Century*. New York: Palgrave Macmillan, 2005.

Tibawi, A.L. *American Interests in Syria, 1800-1901*. Oxford: Clarendon Press, 1966.

Tyrrell, Ian. *Reforming the World: The Creation of America's Moral Empire*. Princeton: Princeton University Press, 2010.

Tuveson, Ernest Lee. *Redeemer Nation: The Idea of America's Millennial Role*. Chicago: The University of Chicago Press, 1968.

U.S. Department of State. *International Religious Freedom Report 2010: Iran*. September 13, 2011 http://www.state.gov/j/drl/rls/irf/2010_5/168264.htm (accessed July 27, 2012).

Van Gorder, Christian A, *Christianity in Persia and the Status of Non-Muslims in Modern Iran*. Lanham: Lexington Books, 2010.

Voice of the Martyrs, *Iran: Desperate for God*. Bartlesville: Living Sacrifice Book Company, 2006.

Washburn, George. *Fifty years in Constantinople and recollections of Robert College*. Boston: Houghton Mifflin Company, 1909.

Weaver, Alain Epp, ed. *Under Vine and Fig Tree: Biblical Theologies of Land and the Palestinian-Israeli Conflict.* Telford: Cascadia Publishing House, 2007.

———. *States of Exile: Visions of Diaspora, Witness, and Return.* Scottsdale: Herald Press, 2008.

Weaver, Alain Epp and Sonia K. Weaver. *Salt & Sign: Mennonite Central Committee in Palestine, 1949-1999.* Akron: Mennonite Central Committee, 1999.

Weigel, George. *American Interest, American Purpose: Moral Reasoning and U.S. Foreign Policy.* Santa Barbara: Praeger Paperback, 1989.

Articles/Chapters

Adalian, Rouben Paul. "The Armenian Genocide." In *Century of Genocide 3rd Edition,* edited by Samuel Totten and William S. Parsons, 55-92. New York: Routledge, 2009.

Akcapar, Sebnem Koser. "Conversion as a Migration Strategy in a Transit Country: Iranian Shiites Becoming Christians in Turkey," *International Migration Review* 40 no. 4 (Winter 2006).

Anderson, Gerald H. "American Protestants in Pursuit of Mission: 1886-1986." *International Bulletin of Missionary Research 12,* no. 3 (July 1988).

Anderson, Rufus. "The Theory of Missions to the Heathen." In *The American National Preacher. Volume 20,* edited by W. H. Bidwell. New York: W. H. Bidwell, 1845.

Baker, Archibald G. "Reactions to the 'Laymen's Report." *The Journal of Religion* 13, no. 4 (October 1933).

Badr, Habib. "American Protestant Missionary Beginning in Beirut and Istanbul: Policy, Politics, Practice and Response." In *New Faith in Ancient Lands: Western Missions in the Middle East in the Nineteenth and Early Twentieth Centuries,* ed. Heleen Murre-van den Berg. Boston: Brill, 2006.

Barton, James L. "The Effect of War on Protestant Missions." *The Harvard Theological Review 12*, no. 1 (January 1919).

———. "The Modern Missionary." *Harvard Theological Review 8*, no. 1 (January 1915).

———. "Reaction of the War upon Islam." *The Journal of Race Development 7*, no. 2 (October 1916).

Barraclough, Steven. "Satellite Television in Iran: Prohibition, Imitation and Reform." *Middle Eastern Studies 37*, no. 3 (July 2001).

Baumgartner, Jody C., Peter L. Francia, and Jonathan S. Morris. "A Clash of Civilizations? The Influence of Religion on Public Opinion of U.S. Foreign Policy in the Middle East." *Political Research Quarterly 61*, no. 2 (June 2008)

Beaver, R. Pierce. "The Legacy of Rufus Anderson." *Occasional Bulletin of Missionary Research 3*, no. 3 (July 1979).

Berger, Peter L. "Four Faces of Global Culture." *The National Interest 49*, (Fall 1997).

Broadcasting Board of Governors. "BBG Research Series Briefing: Iran Media Use 2012." June 12, 2012 http://www.bbg.gov/wp-content/media/2012/06/BBG-Iran-ppt.pdf (accessed July 27, 2012.

Bush, Andrew. "The Implications of Christian Zionism for Mission." *International Bulletin of Missionary Research,* 33.3 (July 2009).

Calafi, Farnaz, Ali Dadpay, and Pouyan Mashayekh. "Iran's Yankee Hero," *The New York Times* (April 18, 2009).

Chambers, William Nesbit to Wilson, December 10, 1915. In *The Papers of Woodrow Wilson, v35 October 1, 1915 – January 27, 1916,* ed. Arthur S. Link. Princeton: Princeton University Press, 1981.

Chapman, Colin. "Time to Give Up the Idea of Christian Mission to Muslims? Some Reflections from the Middle East." *International Bulletin of Missionary Research 28*, no. 3 (July 2004).

Chopra, Anuj. "In Iran, Covert Christian Converts Live With Secrecy and Fear." *U.S. News and World Report* (May 8, 2008). http://www.usnews.com/news/world/articles/2008/05/08/in-iran-covert-christian-converts-live-with-secrecy-and-fear (accessed July 27, 2012).

Dodge, Bayard. "Must There be War in the Middle East," *Reader's Digest 52*, no. 312 (April 1948).

Earle, Edward Mead. "American Missions in the Near East," *Foreign Affairs 7*, no. 3 (April 1929).

Eddy, G. Sherwood. "Can we still believe in foreign missions?" In *Students and the Future of Christian Missions,* edited by Gordon Poteat. New York: Student Volunteer Movement for Foreign Missions, 75-93. 1928.

Handy, Robert T. "The American Religious Depression, 1925-1935." *Church History 29*, no. 1 (March 1960).

Harriet Harris. "Theological Reflections on Religious Resurgence and International Stability: a Look at Protestant Evangelicalism." In *Religion and International Relations* edited by K. R. Dark. New York: St. Martin's Press Inc., 2000.

Huntington, Samuel. "The Clash of Civilizations?" *Foreign Affairs 72*, no. 3 (Summer 1993).

"In Our History: Negotiating Peacetime." *Main Gain: The American University of Beirut Quarterly Magazine 5*, no. 3 (Spring 2007), http://staff.aub.edu.lb/~webmgate/spring2007/article9.htm (accessed September 17, 2011).

Iran Alive Ministries. "Track Record." http://www.iranaliveministries.org/page.aspx?n=16&s=20121323111349&p=Our%20Track%20Record (accessed July 27, 2012).

———. "Vision," http://www.iranaliveministries.org/page.aspx?n=15&s=20121 32 3111335&p=Our%20Vision (accessed July 27, 2012).

Iranian Christians International. "Iranian Evangelical Christians – Some Sociological and Demographic Information" http://www.asylumlaw.org/docs/iran/IRN_3/SEC%20II/Irania n%20Evangelical.pdf (accessed July 27, 2012).

Kerr, David A. "Mission and proselytism: A Middle East perspective." *International Bulletin of Missionary Research 20*, no. 1 (January 1996).

Kling, David W. "The New Divinity and the Origins of the American Board of Commissioners for Foreign Missions" *Church History 27*, no. 4 (December 2003).

Lewis, Bernard. "The Roots of Muslim Rage." *The Atlantic 266*, no. 3 (September 1990).

Lewis, Michael. "The Satellite Subversives." *The New York Times,* (February 24, 2002) http://www.nytimes.com/2002/02/24/magazine/24NITV.html ?pagewanted=all (accessed July 27, 2012).

Murre-van den Berg, Heleen. "The American Board and the Eastern Churches: the 'Nestorian Mission' (1844-1846)." *Orientalia Christiana Periodica 65*, no. 1 (1999)

Mead, Edward Earle. "American Missions in the Near East." *Foreign Affairs 7*, no. 3 (April 1929).

Mead, Walter Russell. "God's Country." *Foreign Affairs 85,* no. 5 (September/October 2006).

Okkenhaug, Inger Marie, ed. *Social Sciences and Missions: Gender and Missions in the Middle East 23*, no. 1 (2010).

Ribuffo, Leo P. "Religion in the History of U.S. Foreign Policy." In *The Influence of Faith: Religious Groups & U.S. Foreign Policy,* edited by Elliot Abrams. Lanham: Rowman & Littlefield Publishers Inc., 2001.

Riley, Jennifer. "Christianity Spreading in Iran via Multimedia." *Christian Today* (June 23, 2007) http://www.christiantoday.com/article/christianity.spreading.i n.iran.via.multimedia/11248.htm (accessed August 10, 2012).

Seiple, Robert. "From Bible Bombardment to Incarnational Evangelism: A Reflection on Christian Witness and Persecution." *The Review of Faith and International Affairs* 7, no. 1 (Spring 2009).

Sharkey, Heather J. "Arabic Antimissionary Treatises: Muslim Responses to Christian Evangelism in the Modern Middle East." *International Bulletin of Missionary Research* 28, no. 3 (July 2004).

Sonne, Paul and Farnaz Fassihi. "In Skies Over Iran, a Battle for Control of Satellite TV" *The Wall Street Journal* (December 27, 2011) http://online.wsj.com/article/SB10001424052970203501304577088380199787036.html (accessed July 27, 2012).

Southeastern Baptist Theological Seminary. "Oral History Interview with Dr. George W. Braswell, Jr." *Southeastern SBC Historical Missiology Oral History Program* (November 28, 2005).

Speer, Robert. "The Personal Worth or Failure of Christianity." In *North American Students and World Advance,* edited by Burton St. John. New York: Student Volunteer Movement for Foreign Missions, 1920.

Talavera, Arturo Fontaine. "Trends Towards Globalization in Chile." In *Many Globalizations: Cultural Diversity in the Contemporary World,* edited by Peter L. Berger and Samuel P. Huntington. Oxford: Oxford University Press, 2002.

"University Challenge: The Future." *The National* (May 8 2009), http://www.thenational.ae/article/20090509/FOREIGN/705089824/1011/FOREIGN (accessed September 17, 2011).

Van Biema, David, Perry Bacon Jr. and Cajmes Carney. "Religion: Missionaries Under Cover," *Time Magazine.* June 30th, 2003. http://www.time.com/time/magazine/article/0,9171,1005107,00.html

Wellman, James K., and Matthew Keyes. "Portable Politics and Durable Religion: The Moral Worldviews of American

Evangelical Missionaries." *Sociology of Religion 68*, no. 4 (Winter 2007).

Woodberry, J. Dudley. "Comparative Witness: Christian Mission and Islamic Da'wah." *The Review of Faith and International Affairs 7*, no. 1 (Spring 2009).

Woodberry, Robert. "Reclaiming the M-Word: The Legacy of Missions in Non-Western Societies." *The Review of Faith and International Affairs 4*, no. 1 (Spring 2006).

World Vision. "World Vision staff, relief aid slated for deadly Iran quake, (December 27, 2012) http://www.worldvision.org/worldvision/pr.nsf/stable/pr_iran _20031227 (accessed August 10, 2012).

Yetkiner, Cemal. "At the Center of the Debate: Bebek Seminary and the Education Policy of the American Board of Commissioners for Foreign Missions (1840-1860)." In *American Missionaries and the Middle East: Foundation Encounters,* ed. Mehmet Ali Doğan and Heather J. Sharkey. Salt Lake City: University of Utah Press, 2011.

Zirinsky, Michael. "American Presbyterian Missionaries at UrmiaDuring the Great War," *Proceedings of the International Roundtable on Persia and the Great War,* Tehran, 2-3 March 1997

———. "Render Therefore Unto Caesar the Things Which Are Caesar's: American PresbyterianEducators and Reza Shah." *Iranian Studies 26.3/4* (Summer – Autumn 1993).

Annual Reports

ABCFM. *1836 Annual Report.* Boston, 1366.

———. 1916.

———. 1918.

———. 1919.

———. 1920.

————. 1923.

————. 1924.

————. 1939.

————. 1932.

————. 1942.

————.1960.

BFMPC. *1914 Annual Report.* New York: BFMPC, 1914.

————. 1916.

————. 1919.

————. 1922.

————. 1941.

Index